Letters
from the
Med

To the late Ian and Geraldine Treleaven for teaching us to appreciate the love of the sea.

summer cruising

Letters

under the

from the

endless sun

Med

ANDREA & IAN TRELEAVEN

NEW HOLLAND

CONTENTS

Introduction

You get only one life but plenty of dreams to fulfil. This was just one of our dreams – to acquire a yacht in the Mediterranean and slowly cruise back to Australia. Three years later we have still not left the Med. In 2003, surfing the Web, we spotted a one-year-old Beneteau Oceanis 473 yacht sitting in a marina in Spain, and we purchased it through Beneteau Vicsail, Sydney. Our plans evolved: now we would spend half a year in the European summer and half back in Australia, living an endless summer for a few years.

About us

We decided to make the break for Europe after selling a successful nautical clothing business, which served Australia and New Zealand with brands such as Musto and Line 7, as well as licensed clothing for the 2000 Olympic Games.

Ian, who grew up in Christchurch, New Zealand, already had a lot of miles under his belt, coming from a sailing family. His father was president of the New Zealand Yachting Federation and his brother an Olympic yachtsman. Starting out with his own dinghy at age seven, Ian represented New Zealand in the Laser class and later was bowman on the 1973 US Admiral's Cup team yacht *Salty Goose*. He has taught sailing at Club Med Martinique and worked for Derektors boatyard in New York. He has participated in many Sydney–Hobart races and added records to his name. During a two-handed race from Sydney to Auckland in 1988 on *Starlight Express* he was hit by Cyclone Bola, surviving to tell the tale. Ian has also campaigned his own yachts including the Volvo Ocean 60 Merit for which he still holds the 420 nm Lord Howe Island Ocean Race record.

As for me, I grew up Andrea Hockly, daughter of Alison and Ian, in Te Awamutu in New Zealand's North Island. Before meeting Ian Treleaven I had travelled widely in Europe. Ian introduced me to sailing and I have loved it ever since, although most of the time I supported him from the sidelines, keeping business and family together.

I had no previous experience in writing or photography but developed the skills in the Med and wrote a weekly newsletter to friends. This expanded to 'Treleavens' Travels' through Di Pearson, then editor of www.sail-world.com, as a weekly feature on her website. I had always dreamed of writing a book and took note of this comment in a letter from Janey: 'I wish you the best with a book ... One piece of advice: write what you would want to read.'

About the boat

We have been very pleased with our Beneteau 473 (47 feet). Voluminous for her size, she's spacious enough down below for extended living, but not too large for two people to handle. She sails well in all conditions, and has an excellent sail wardrobe with extras in a staysail and spinnaker. The big Yanmar 75HP engine also makes life comfortable. The only disadvantage is that we are in the upper rating band when it comes to berthage fees, where they rate us by length and beam. Serious sailing buffs can look up the yacht's specs on page 47.

Tips on cruising

Through the book you'll find notes from Ian that cover a range of topics, from making visa paperwork easier to dealing with local customs, sailing hints, tips on mooring or anchoring, appraisals of nifty gizmos we picked up, and other items that we hope will make life easier for anyone planning to visit the region under canvas, whether by chartered or private yacht. References in the text to 'miles' are nautical miles (2025 yards or 1.85 km).

Currency

Most European countries have accepted the euro as their denomination, which makes things highly convenient. Over the three years covered in the book the euro rate varied. From about .55 to the Australian dollar (.50 to the New Zealand dollar) it rose to .62 (.59).

Tips on food

In the book I offer recipes for a few of the meals we've enjoyed in various countries. Where possible we use local ingredients, and they're all tailored to cooking on board. Cooking at sea has taught me the art of simplicity. Everything on the boat is small – oven, two-burner stove, pantry and galley – and I have no fancy gadgets. I improvise: vegetables are parboiled and left to steam-cook in plastic containers with the lid on. I may be cooking for six or more people, so instead of serving individual meals I set out dishes in the centre on the table.

Food shopping in the Med is mind-blowing, as there is always something different from one country to the next. Look for whatever is local and seasonal, as it will be full of flavour and probably cheaper too. This goes for wine and honey as well as bread, pastries, fruit, vegetables and cheeses, which are often just as good in the supermarkets as in local street stalls. Olive trees are everywhere, so I use lashings of extra virgin oil, along with garlic and lemon. Meat can be limited but you can usually get chicken, pork and mince – though there's no pork in Muslim countries like Tunisia. Lamb can be hard to find, especially in Spain, and ditto for fillet steak. If I find good meat I usually buy enough for a few days. The names of cold cuts can be confusing: prosciutto and Parma ham are the same thing, namely thin-sliced, cured ham. Herbs and spices are delicious. Many, such as rosemary and fennel, grow wild. I tend to stock up mostly on dried herbs but always buy a fresh basil plant.

Some other local specialities include:
Spain Sheep's cheese; Spanish melons (green and football-shaped); cured ham; baby cos lettuce;
Italy Parmesan cheese in lovely huge, inexpensive blocks; pasta fresh and dried in a wonderful variety of types; marinated anchovies; sun-dried tomatoes; buffalo mozzarella; barbecued artichoke hearts;
Sardinia Thin dried bread; salami;
Sicily Wild flowers; coloured pasta, pesto, raisin and onion relish; Marsala;

France *Coquelet* (a small chicken); cheese, cheese and more cheese; raspberries, mussels, salami and other cured meats; frankly everything;
Corsica Cream caramels;
Tunisia Herbs and spices; fish; seasonal fruit and veggies;
Malta English goods: baked beans, mint sauce, HP sauce;
Greece Feta cheese; nougat; yogurt;
Croatia Deep-fried seafood; truffles in season; wild asparagus in season;
Turkey Turkish delight, of course; feta; nuts and dried fruit; mild to hot chillies in season; sun-dried tomatoes.

Why we do it

Over three summers we have sailed 8000 miles and visited 11 countries. At the time of writing this, we're off to continue our travels and revisit favourite places. We've fallen in love with the Mediterranean, from Europe and Turkey to Africa. We get a completely new perspective from the sea where everywhere is more accessible – no airports, no hotels and no baggage. We've learned a huge amount in our three summers (so far) in the Mediterranean, from on-board technology to maintaining the yacht, from navigation (using GPS via the laptop) to the dive compressor that we use when cleaning the hull.

One of the great joys has been sharing experiences – with our daughter and son Janey and Ian (both in their twenties) for several weeks of each year; with old friends who join us on board; and with new acquaintances who are doing exactly what we are doing. To quote from a letter written by friend Sabrina Snow, who with her husband George joined us on our 2005 cruise:

'How wonderful to get your email this morning about St Tropez! ... Your words brought it all back, that bright sunshine, clear turquoise water, balmy days sipping mojitos and smooth Italian wines, one day sliding into the next in a Mediterranean idyll of fun times, good food and good company ...'

Although we were too young to stop work we believed it important to live our dream while we were still fit enough. We are all much fitter than our parents were at this age, and you can always return to the workforce later in life. Hopefully this book will convince others to seize the chance, when it's presented, to live out a dream.

Andrea Treleaven, May 2006

CÁDIZ TO ROME

Cádiz

We arrive in Cádiz, Spain, on the Atlantic coast 60 miles north of Gibraltar, on the last Friday in July 2003. In the marina Puerto Sherry we take possession of our near-new Beneteau 473 Oceanis Clipper. After 37 hours of travelling, it's a shock to find her covered in red dust with barnacles on the hull. The dust has blown in from Africa. No one here washes their boat: there's no point. But down below we find her immaculate and fully equipped. We clean and scrub, getting ready to relaunch her as *Cádiz*, named after the place where our adventure begins. There's no real agenda for our first season, other than to sail into the Med, up the coast of Spain, to the Balearic Islands and across to Sardinia and Corsica, then winter her in Italy while we return to a Sydney summer.

The ISAF world sailing pre-Olympics championships are here in September, and already we are catching up with New Zealanders and Aussies in training. Barbara Kendall and husband Shayne Bright, with two-year-old Samantha, bring champagne and – a sailing tradition – a toy treasure chest, filled with chocolate coins to give the pirates for luck. (We still have the treasure chest on board, as we hadn't seen any pirates to date.) Also on board are Olympian Aaron McIntosh and partner Jay-Jay Snider with two-year-old Daniella, so our first sail will be in fine company.

It is Europe's hottest summer and the sea breeze certainly helps. With the Atlantic at its doorstep, the seafood market early every morning is a hive of activity. We soon get used to taking siestas between 2 pm and 5 pm, when all the shops shut and everyone goes home for a leisurely lunch and a sleep. So civilised. The evenings are spent enjoying the local produce as this area is famous for its sherry, port and balsamic vinegar. Six of us jam into a Fiat and head into El Puerto de Santa Maria to dine at Di Faro, with its fantastic entrance of old carved doors, Spanish tapestries and local produce. At 9.30 pm we think we're late, but by Spanish standards we're early. Ian doesn't miss a beat: orders food, wine, gets down to conversation and eyes every girl that enters. Not to worry, the men look pretty good too.

We're stuck in port because of the Levanter winds. They're hot, last up to 10 days, and can blow 30-plus knots relentlessly. Our son Ian is due in Gibraltar soon to stay with us for two weeks, so we're keen to leave. Travelling in 30 knots doesn't worry us but we'll be heading straight into the wind and getting around Tarifa Point can be hard.

By chance El Puerto de Santa Maria is home to a famous bull ring, so off we go. Amid the gold braid, pageantry and posturing, the music, clapping and shouts of 'Olé!', it all comes down to 20 minutes in the ring and silence as the bull is killed with great skill. Now it's up to the crowd to approve, waving white *banderos* and clapping. The mayor decides that two ears are to be cut off and it's all cheers, the ears are tossed into the crowd – not near us, luckily! Three matadors and six bulls later, it's a tie between two matadors, who are paraded on shoulders with their costumes of gold and white now spattered with blood. I wonder if a Spaniard watching a rugby match in Sydney would come away as bewildered as we are. We buy steak the next day, and it just isn't the same.

Another day in port, so we catch a train to explore the city. Ian is like a dog that follows long brown legs and tight skirts. (All good dogs know they go home to eat.) The city of Cádiz, with its narrow streets, towering façades and wrought ironwork, is 3000 years old. It was Spain's main port for ships sailing for America. Christopher Columbus left from here, so we are in good company. Almost an island, the city has beautiful white beaches, one of which is El Puerto de Santa Maria and its new port Puerto Sherry. Everyone seems to own a sun umbrella, deck chair and Vespa. The entire family – Mum, Dad, kids – pile on the one Vespa and head to the beach, no helmets.

Topiary, Cádiz

The other Cádiz

CÁDIZ
SYDNEY

There's no real agenda for our first season, other than to sail into the Med, up the coast of Spain, to the Balearic Islands and across to Sardinia and Corsica, then winter her in Italy . . .

Airport and marina, Gibraltar

Cádiz to Gibraltar

It's time we were off. In frustration we leave for the tuna-fishing port of Barbate, on our first sail down the coast. With Dean Martin singing 'One man, one wife, one love through life' on the stereo, we try to set sail in 25–30 knots, but it's on the nose and we have to motor 35 nautical miles. It's beautifuly cool and fresh. We watch out for the tuna nets that can lie 2 kilometres straight out from the coast, as well as the inflatable beach mattresses and beach balls that have blown off the beaches. It's a long, slow day passing Cape Trafalgar and we think of battles won and lost here.

It doesn't pay to make any plans when it comes to cruising on boats – the weather will play an important part and we'll always have to be flexible. Holed up here in Barbate are a lot of boats, cruisers and yachts of all sizes trying to get to Gibraltar. When you ask when the wind will die down, you only get a shrug and a very daunting 'Could last another 10 days.' If only we could get around the corner then the easterly will be good for us.

We've had two days in port and our son flies into Gibraltar, so it's our first experience of finding a bus timetable and going overland to bring him back to Barbate. The three of us leave early the next morning before the wind comes in too strong and head for Gibraltar. In the night the boat was hit by a sandstorm, a new experience for us but not surprising, as Europe is having their highest temperatures in 60 years.

Wind on the nose, we motor around Tarifa Point, famous for windsurfers and kite boarders – and we see hundreds, looking like butterflies loving the fresh winds in all their fluoro colours. Our first major port and formalities are surprisingly informal, held in a shed on a pontoon with kids fishing off it and Customs only interested in stowaways.

Visiting Gibraltar is like popping into an English port, and it's fun being able to speak English and feel normal again. Apparently it's a good place to get things fixed, but it's August and everyone is on holiday (we later found that it was cheaper to provision the boat in southern Spain). The history is great, the views from the top of the rock impressive and I love the amphitheatre in the rock that's still used for concerts. The apes are something else! One points the way to go and two ambush us to steal young Ian's ice cream. After a warm English beer and cold pie, we are happy to move on, but have to come back later for more in-boat gadgets to be installed.

Gibraltar to Morocco and back again

Not a lot happens in Gibraltar on Sunday, so we take a trip across the strait to Morocco. It's fantastic that in four hours or so you can be on another continent, with culture and food so very different. We decide to sail down the east coast to a small fishing port called Smir, but it is not to be. Near the coast we hit thick sea mist, with visibility at only 10 feet – scary since we're among small fishing boats with nets out that don't register on the radar. We can hear the *thump-thump* of marine diesels but have no sense of where they are. It's all too much for my nerves, so we turn back to Ceuta.

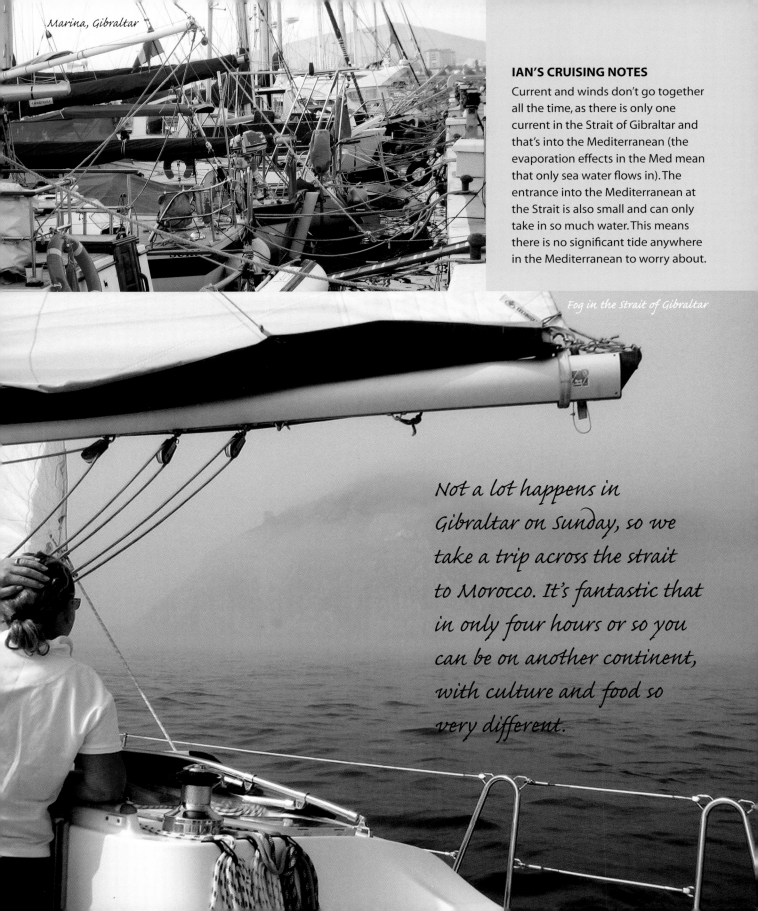

Marina, Gibraltar

IAN'S CRUISING NOTES

Current and winds don't go together all the time, as there is only one current in the Strait of Gibraltar and that's into the Mediterranean (the evaporation effects in the Med mean that only sea water flows in). The entrance into the Mediterranean at the Strait is also small and can only take in so much water. This means there is no significant tide anywhere in the Mediterranean to worry about.

Fog in the Strait of Gibraltar

Not a lot happens in Gibraltar on Sunday, so we take a trip across the strait to Morocco. It's fantastic that in only four hours or so you can be on another continent, with culture and food so very different.

Spice market, Ceuta

Ceuta is still Spanish and on the northernmost point of Morocco. As soon as we hit the dock, the tour guides are there to haggle, and we hire one to take us to the town of Tétouan with its old bazaar. One thing we do is buy spices – the fragrance is tantalising and I can't wait to cook with them. We return, dust ourselves off and sample some local food to end the day on a good note.

Ceuta is still Spanish and on the northernmost point of Morocco. As soon as we hit the dock, the tour guides are there to haggle and we hire one to take us to the town of Tétouan with its old bazaar and cafés full of men dressed in grey. The old Mercedes has no air-conditioning, no seat belts and a breakneck driver – we're in shock and awe. Our guide wants us to shop till we drop, but we just want a look around. Lucky for Ian I have no need for carpets, silver teapots or leatherware on a boat. Shopping for electronics is very good here, and it's duty-free. One thing we do buy is spices – the fragrance is tantalising and I can't wait to cook with them. We return, dust ourselves off and sample some Moroccan food to end the day on a good note. August is not a month to be here: it's a soup of hot, dry, dusty fog.

I'm fascinated by the diets of different countries and their health properties. The diet here is high in protein. Fish is in abundance: fresh or dried, coated with spices, grilled or just deep-fried. Not to mention marinated or deep-fried octopuses, grilled prawns in salt, deep-fried squid, spiced meat on small skewers barbecued over coals. It's a simple diet, and the people look healthy and not overweight.

We stay an extra night to dine on the waterfront at El Reflecto and haven't a clue what we order (no English menu), but it's all fresh fish and enjoyed by all. By 10 pm the fog has enveloped us, and the atmosphere at the marina is eerie.

It's a strange feeling to wake surrounded in fog while it's still very hot. We set off back to Gibraltar, but with visibility nil and ferries and container ships everywhere, we nearly turn back as the radar screen looks like it's full of train carriages. Halfway across the fog lifts and dolphins lead us into Gibraltar.

Spain, Gibraltar, Morocco, Spain, all in a few days, with everyone wanting to stamp our passports and sight the boat papers and insurance documents. I guess we'll get used to it.

IAN'S CRUISING NOTES

The yacht came with a radar and we had a quick lesson in using it in the fog crossing to Morocco. Radar is a must, as fog is common in this area due to climatic changes. We found it comforting to locate vessels on the radar 200 metres away that we could hear but not see. We taught ourselves to use it by plotting ships during daylight. We use the radar extensively on our few night passages in the Med, plotting other vessels continuously and monitoring their course in relation to ours. Most ships steer around us, so our radar reflector must be very effective. Amazingly, during 8500 miles sailed in three years we've had only 13 nights at sea. Everything in the Med is so close that we can easily do 80 miles in daylight, even under motor.

By the marina at Ceuta is a great market for provisioning the boat with fresh fish and vegetables, which we've made a note of for when we cross the Atlantic for the Caribbean.

RECIPES **SPAIN**

MOROCCAN SCAMPI

2 Tbsp olive oil
3 cloves garlic, crushed
½ cup dry sherry
½ cup tomato purée
12 scampi, shell on
dash of hot chilli sauce
    (optional)

In a pan, heat oil and garlic, then
stir in sherry and tomato purée.
Add scampi and cook for 6 minutes,
turning over from time to time.
Remove from heat and let sauce
reduce by about 20%. Add chilli sauce
to taste if desired. Pour sauce over
scampi and serve with French bread.

MELON WITH PROSCIUTTO

My favourite lunch – simple, cool and
refreshing. Spanish melons are dark
green and shaped like a rugby ball. You
can also use cantaloupe or honeydew.

1 whole Spanish melon, cut in half
    lengthwise, seeds scooped
    out, and then each half cut into
    6 wedges and rind removed
150 g prosciutto, thinly sliced and
    cut into 25 mm strips
100 g sheep's cheese, thinly sliced
splash of extra virgin olive oil
    (optional)

Place melon wedges on a platter, then
drape with sliced prosciutto and cheese.
Drizzle with oil if desired.

EGG AND PARMA HAM SALAD

2 baby cos lettuces, washed
    and shredded
2 eggs, hard-boiled, each
    cut into 8 pieces
4 artichoke hearts, halved
4 slices Parma ham, cut into strips
handful of fresh mint,
    coarsely chopped
juice of 1 lemon
¼ cup extra virgin olive oil
sea salt and freshly cracked black
    pepper

In a salad bowl, toss together lettuce,
egg, artichokes, ham and mint. Sprinkle
lemon juice and oil over salad, and
season to taste.

La Duquesa

Gibraltar to Caleta de Velez

We finally leave for the Costa del Sol, the gateway to the Mediterranean. There are 320 days of sun a year here and not a breath of wind, so it's dead calm all the way to Puerto de la Duquesa. On the way we stop in a bay, Cala Sardina – what fun to be able to choose your anchorage at whim and swim off the boat for the first time in the deliciously warm sea. It's mid-August and we are finally cruising in the Mediterranean, the sea is sparkling and the feeling of coming into this huge enclosed waterway is great.

We berth at the marina Puerto de la Duquesa. Unusually, Ian's taking a long time cleaning the decks this evening; I call it perving while you work. Hopping ashore to dine at Bar Domingo, we sit outside and enjoy seafood with a thousand cats and locals. Ian gets cross when I try to feed some of the stray cats under the table, but their little begging eyes are irresistible. A delicacy here is fried baby squid, undersized by Australian standards but irresistible. The 'new Spanish' style architecture – painted white archways, orange tile roofs – and pink bougainvilleas make for a perfect holiday destination.

Next day it's 40°C and still no wind, so we motor on to Puerto de Jose Banus. This is casino Costa del Sol, the best and most popular port on the Spanish coast. We phone ahead to book a berth, only to be told it's booked out. Taking a chance, we call in anyway and after some negotiation we are

Puerto de Jose Banus

Next day it's 40°C and still no wind, so we motor on to Puerto de Jose Banus. This is casino Costa del Sol, the best and most popular port on the Spanish coast. We phone ahead to book a berth, but it's booked out.

Frigiliana

squeezed in. Port fees at €70 a night are very high, but it certainly lives up to expectations. When we ask for laundry facilities, the reply is 'Why wash when you have all these shops?' Every fashion house of Europe is here with world-class shop fitouts. Then, of course, the new clothes have to be worn, so the evenings are one big parade along the promenade in front of hundreds of mega boats, from the Prince of Saudi's huge cruiser down to our little 47-footer. We drink in the atmosphere, eat dinner and watch the entertainment – long legs, peeping bottoms and brown navels.

The wind has picked up from the west and it's nice to finally get the sails up – we set a course for Puerto Caleta de Velez and the autopilot takes over the steering. It's like having another person on board, but you still have to watch for the craypot buoys that dot the coast.

We contact a friend of a friend living in Caleta de Velez, and in true Aussie style it's 'Come for a barbecue!' Lovely to make contact with people living in the area. Jane from Australia is married to an Englishman, David Earle, who has lived here for 20 years. A lot of English people are coming to live here now – it's a great lifestyle with a long hot summer and skiing in the Sierra Nevada only two hours away. We plan to stay here a few days and take in some of the countryside. With Jane and David we visit picture-postcard Frigiliana, a white-painted village in a mountain valley with narrow lanes, lots of white stairs and hanging pink bougainvillea.

After refuelling with a Spanish summer wine (half red wine and half soda) and delicious tapas, we dine at a private villa overlooking Frigiliana. The owner, Pepe, has a well-stocked cellar and we sample homegrown muscatel wine straight from the barrels. This is just for starters – after more wine, squid on the barbecue, and young Ian's 21st birthday cake, we all gaze at the fairy lights of Frigiliana twinkling in the distance.

Another day is spent at Torre de Mar, lining up for a

Marina del Este, Costa del Sol

IAN'S CRUISING NOTES

Marina fees along the Spanish coast started off at about €30 a night, including water and electricity, increasing in price and becoming busier as we went further north. At Puerto Banus we paid €70 for the last one available, but that was an exception. On Formentera they were €175 a night! Needless to say, we anchored out. Sailing up the Spanish coast, we spent every night in a marina as the prevailing winds made it impossible to stay in a sheltered bay. As we sailed east anchorages were more freely available, but we still spent half our time in marinas to enjoy local life ashore.

Frigiliana with son Ian

Alhambra palace

seafood lunch with the locals at a bar/restaurant on the beach, and being caught out again by the three-hour siesta that begins at 2 pm. As we are originally New Zealanders, we're excited to see whitebait and scallops on the menu. It's wonderful to sit at the bar and order great seafood, from steamed cockles to squid rings, have a beer and relax in this very hot weather. At the local yacht club the barbecue is a makeshift wooden dinghy, filled with sand and housing a small fire on which sardines are grilled on skewers.

Well, occasionally you just have to be a tourist, and we want to see the Alhambra. Tickets are hard to come by and the only way now is to take a day tour by bus. It's stiflingly hot – nearly 40°C by the time we're picked up at the marina at 7.30 am. Our tour time into the palace is 3.30 pm – everyone has a set time to enter, which means no queuing or crowds as you go through. It's a very good system, and we follow our fan-waving guide all day.

The Alhambra is Spain's top tourist attraction, with 8000 visitors a day, and is one of the finest achievements of Islamic architecture in the world. The palace is lavishly decorated with intricate stone and wood carvings, and geometric tile patterns on most of the ceilings, walls and floors. I visited 30 years ago and am still amazed at the irrigation of the Generalife gardens, flourishing after 1000 years.

We also visited the Royal Chapel in beautiful Granada, viewing the iron caskets of King Fernando and Queen Isabel, who expelled the Moors from the last of their strongholds in Granada, and funded Christopher Columbus' explorations. A great day all round, made so easy by taking the bus.

Anchored off Caleta de Velez

IAN'S CRUISING NOTES

After hooking several nets around the propeller, we decided it was time to purchase dive gear and did so in Torrevieja. Dive bottles are too heavy and difficult to fill unless you are a certified diver, but by pure chance we found the one and only Australian-made deck compressor looking lonely in a Spanish chandlery. You attach it to your batteries, put on the regulator and down you go to 10 metres for up to an hour. As luck would have it we haven't hooked much since, but it's great to clean the bottom and fun to dive with. The first year the water was 10 per cent warmer and a lot of barnacles grew. I use it more to help other yachts in trouble with ropes on propellers and dirty bottoms, or finding articles dropped over the side.

On this leg, we gave our yellow spinnaker its maiden outing, and it was exciting to experience a little speed. But by the end of the first day it was blowing 30 knots and a heart-stopping experience getting the spinnaker down; quickly we stuffed it below decks to sort out later. We decided there and then to have a spinnaker sock (which makes it easier to contain) at the earliest opportunity.

Caleta de Velez to Costa Blanca

Young Ian reluctantly flies home to Sydney, but we will sail on up the coast. As we leave Puerto Caleta de Velez, Jane swims out with a mobile phone tied atop her head and joins us for a short sail. The diving in this area is fantastic. Small coves and nudist beaches dot the coast with their open-air beach bars; if Ian has his way we will visit them all.

We read, write, sunbathe and sometimes do the dishes. We're learning to relax, taking all day to go 35 miles, but we will keep up some speed to get to Ibiza in the Balearics. The countryside has turned from apartment blocks to barren land and plastic-covered market gardens. What's grown here feeds northern Europe: impressive but no pretty picture. Anchoring on this exposed stretch is not so easy either, but thankfully marinas dot the coast every 30 miles.

Entering Motril our propeller picks up a stray piece of net. Ian dives to free it, but the barnacles on the hull inflict a deep cut on his finger. There's blood all over, and though I'm squeamish I patch him up before we head out to sea again.

The sight of local Parma ham, sheep cheese, olive oil, olives and a BYO-wine-container shop (where wine is cheaper than water) was wonderful at the small fishing village of Adra, where we arrived late and tied up next to the fishing boats on the wharf for free (often not allowed). The next night is in Almerimar, where it's cheap and good for long-stayers.

Rounding Cabo de Gata, the depth sounder registered just 1 metre – that panicked us until we realised the water is so deep that it doesn't register! We pass barren but interesting rock formations, as well as ruins of castles and towers left by the Moors in the 12th century. The Moors built square forts and towers, and later the Spanish built round structures, but they are all in natural stone and very handy for navigation.

After hooking more fishing net and again having to use snorkel gear to free the propeller from the rope, weights and net, we resolve to buy dive equipment soon. Ian, having swallowed half the harbour, vomits and shits for the next hour while I motor on to Cartagena.

Entering Cartagena is an extraordinary experience, a time warp. Hills surround the port and on every high point stands a lookout tower, fort or castle. At night these are lit up and at first glance you think there's something in the sky. The history here dates back to 200 BC, and we are impressed by the first submarine sitting as a monument on the dock, built and designed by Cartagena-born Isaac Peral in 1884. The city mixes modern buildings with elaborate old architecture.

The next day we sail past Mar Menor, a huge inland salt-water lake that looks like Surfer's Paradise from the water. Torrevieja, home of impressive pyramids of salt, turns out to have a helpful English-speaking nautical shop, named Oliver's after a resident cat, and we purchase a dive compressor. Up until now, food has been about the same price as home, but wine is bottom-dollar and it's become a game to see who can find the cheapest bottle.

At Alicante the amazing Costelo Barbara perches on a hill overlooking the city. The entrance to the castle is a walk along a tunnel into the hill and up by lift (a relief in this heat). The marina is the most expensive so far, at €80 for one night, so Ian uses all his sales skills and talks us into the private yacht club. Our membership of the CYCA (Cruising Yacht Club of Australia) has to come in handy now and again. The Real Club Alicante is upmarket and welcoming, but don't count on getting a marina space – that area is 'members only'.

Sam, our white cat at home, has had to be put down. He has been buried in the garden under his favourite chair overlooking the Sydney Harbour. Janey also has her tonsils out and as a mother I find it hard not to be there, but she will be with us in six weeks and we look forward to that.

Sailing from Alicante to Javea, we anchor for the night at the closest point to sail out to Ibiza tomorrow.

The sight of local Parma ham, sheep cheese, olive oil, olives and a BYO-wine-container shop was wonderful at the small fishing village of Adra, where we arrived late and tied up next to the fishing boats on the wharf for free.

RECIPES **SPAIN**

CINNAMON CHICKEN AND WHITE BEAN SALAD

Fresh mint adds zing to this salad, but you can use dried if the fresh herb isn't available.

1½ Tbsp extra virgin olive oil
2 boneless, skinless chicken breasts, each cut in half horizontally
1 tsp ground cinnamon
2 Tbsp brown sugar
⅓ cup sherry

In a pan, heat oil and add chicken pieces. Sprinkle with cinnamon and sugar and sauté for 1–2 minutes on each side. Add sherry and allow sauce to reduce for a few minutes. Do not overcook chicken.

WHITE BEAN SALAD

1 can white beans or chickpeas, drained
2 small tomatoes, cut into small chunks
1 Spanish red onion, peeled and diced
small handful fresh mint, coarsely chopped
1 clove garlic, peeled and crushed
¼ cup apple cider vinegar

Combine ingredients in a bowl and marinate for 1 hour.

Transfer salad to a platter and arrange cooked, warm chicken pieces on top. Use excess sauce in pan as a dressing.

CHICKEN 'PUERTO SHERRY'

2 Tbsp olive oil
2 Tbsp butter
2 boneless skinless chicken breasts, each cut in half horizontally
1 Tbsp Dijon mustard
2 cloves garlic, peeled and finely chopped
½ cup sherry, sweet or dry
1 Tbsp brown sugar (only required if using dry sherry)
½ cup milk or cream
chopped parsley to garnish

Heat oil and butter in pan and sauté chicken pieces until cooked through, about 2–3 minutes each side. Remove from pan and set aside. Set heat to low and add to pan mustard, garlic, sherry, sugar if using and milk. Heat to a low simmer but do not boil, stirring occasionally. Return chicken pieces to pan and warm through (do not overcook chicken). Place chicken pieces on platter and pour sauce over. Sprinkle with chopped parsley and serve.

Ibiza

After an early start and never losing sight of land, we sail 55 miles to Puerto San Antonio under a clear blue sky. We arrive to 40°C heat, beautiful bays and white-sand beaches, and wall-to-wall people. The clarity and depth of the water are amazing, and we can't wait to swim. Because of accidents, swimming areas are now ringed with yellow buoys to keep out all motorboats. We're anchored in the middle of the harbour but with the sound of discos all around, we may be in for a long night.

San Antonio is very much a place for young hippies, so we move on. Our first bay, Cala Badella, is not to be missed. The deep blue sea turns to gorgeous turquoise on the sandy beaches (which are surprisingly clean, despite the tourists).

We have come south to sail around Ibiza (the island) and cross to Puerto Sabina on the island of Formentera, south of Ibiza (the city); more gorgeous beaches and thousands of boats, a real 'boys' toys' area. The young and old flock here, and it's nudist country too. Vespas are in their thousands and are the way to see the island, but we leave that to the young ones. The sunsets are fantastic, and Ibiza marks the beginning of our nonstop holiday with barely a breath of wind or a shower of rain for 90 days.

In from the beach are natural sulphuric mud pools. You coat your body from head to toes, walk to the beach to let it dry hard, then wash it all off in the sea. The mud bath exfoliates the skin and leaves you feeling fantastic, but the smell lingers for a few days. A small price for eternal youth.

A refreshing spell of rain brings a quick burst of thunder and lightning. The kids on the boat next to us dance in the rain and everyone is out with their brooms scrubbing the decks. But that evening electrical storms start, so it's out of bed in the middle of the night to re-anchor and then put a second anchor down. This place is notorious for bad holding, having had thousands of boats moor here during the summer and plough up the bottom. There are 25 boats in the bay and half of them are in trouble, so you also have to watch that no one is dragging into you. Our dinghy flips with the outboard still on, shoes and oars gone, over and over it goes. There are now two boats on the beach, only metres from the rocks.

Next morning we decide to up anchor and leave, but a big black cloud and lightning changes all that. Without warning, driving rain and wind tear out of the east at 50 knots and all hell breaks loose. While righting our overturned inflatable (again), I look into the stinging rain to see a 50-footer from Holland bearing down on us; one of her two fin rudders wraps around our anchor lines. Crashing down our side and nearly tangling the rigs, she is now dragging us towards the beach.

Ian goes forward and, bridging the language barrier with lots of arm-waving and f-words, assesses what can be done. With the motor on and in full throttle, I'm trying to stop us from grounding. Then Ian, with sheer guts, lets go one of the anchor lines and flicks it out and back, securing our own boat again.

We ride out the storm, just metres from four yachts aground on the beach. Anchors, chain and rope everywhere, we sort out the mess and leave very quickly while the coastguard comes in to clean up. We later heard the storm was so severe that Ibiza airport was closed for two hours, a first in years. Cumulus clouds were forming in the north but the weather had not been predicted by anyone. These little surprises do happen in the Med, so I make a mental note to keep an eye on those clouds. Despite all this, we are having a wonderful time.

I have a firm rule: no yelling at me when I drop the anchor. I see a lot of men yell at the wife when the anchoring doesn't go to plan, and they're effectively announcing to the whole bay that the wife just mucked up. I use hand signals, so when the marked chain is 10 metres out I show one finger, 40 metres out I show four fingers, and so on. I also have some other finger signals in case he does embarrass me.

Approaching San Antonio, Ibiza

Mud baths, Isla Espalmador

In from the beach are natural sulphuric mud pools. You coat your body from head to toes, walk to the beach to let it dry hard, then wash it all off in the sea. The mud bath exfoliates the skin and leaves you feeling fantastic, but the smell lingers for a few days.

Isla de Formentera

IAN'S CRUISING NOTES

At Club Nautico de Ibiza I decided to get the scratches polished out from the recent storm, and employed someone to do the work. Here we learnt a trick the hard way: sometimes workmen turn up with empty containers of polish, watch you leave for the day and proceed to do nothing until you come back later. When you point out that there's no improvement, they insist you look at how much polish they used. It's a very expensive lesson – never leave your boat while people are working on it.

It's a good idea to have communication on board, but Internet cafés are everywhere and a lot cheaper in the Med. We chose not to have a satellite phone as they are expensive to buy and run. We used my Australian Telstra mobile phone and a Hotmail email account to keep in contact with everyone. During our third year, we used the mobile to access the Internet. The service is getting better and less expensive each year. The Internet also made access to news easy while we were in the Med; we checked the **Sydney Morning Herald** (www.smh.com.au), **New Zealand Herald** (www.nzherald.co.nz), and **Sail World** (www.sail-world.com) for sailing news. On the HF radio we got BBC World Service.

We took all the photos on two Sony digital still cameras – a DSC-F828 (8 mega-pixel) and a DSC-T3 Cybershot (5.1 mega-pixel). We downloaded each night through a Sony Gate Mouse – which holds the memory stick – onto our Toshiba Tecra laptop, which runs off the yacht's 12-volt system.

After the storms it's a rough trip to Ibiza (the city), but worth getting into a harbour and tying up at Club Nautico, a marina in need of repair. The wharf sits at an angle of 30 degrees, only 30 centimetres above water level, and passing ferries cause quite a wash. Could be interesting getting Ian home at night after a few drinks! At €60 a night it's luck if you can get in – your only options are very upmarket marinas at twice the price and miles from the centre.

Meanwhile, Ian has to get the outboard fixed. He delivers it to the local repair shop on a wheelbarrow he's found. At first they say it'll take 'days to fix', but then they find we're not English but Australian, and it's ready that afternoon.

We love Ibiza city for its pretty people and restaurants set in cobbled lanes. It's a wonderful place with lots of history and a wonderfully preserved old town, cathedral and fortress. Ibiza is now on UNESCO's World Heritage List, and its four elements sum up the essence of the island: the walled side of Dalt Vila; the Necropolis of Puig des Molins; the Phoenician settlement; and the fields of *Posidonia oceanica* (seagrass). The shopping and nightlife are the best in Europe, but nothing starts till 3 am so we flag the partying. There is something for everyone, you just have to find your own level.

A sign on the local yacht club's door insists that clothing must be worn. On our way back to the boat at 1 am, we are confronted by the Guardia Civile at a roped-off area. Anyone trying to get through to the nightclubs is threatened with handcuffs. After waiting patiently for an hour, we hear two explosions, and are finally allowed on the boat at 4 am. We hear the next day it was a bomb scare, and the doors were blown open on a suspect's car in the yacht club car park.

We move to the top of the island and prepare to sail across to Majorca, anchoring in Cala Portinatx for the night as this is the shortest point to cross from. An English couple, Jenny and Phillip, are living on board a self-built 50-footer and about to winter in Majorca, finding whatever work they can and sailing on again next season. What a life! One thing you notice is how healthy everyone who's sailing looks – not just tanned but lean and fit too. Jenny and Phillip give us RTTY, a computer program to get free weather information on the HF radio in English from Germany.

Majorca

On first approach Majorca looks fantastic, and to date we haven't changed our opinion. This is paradise with sophistication – the water is at 27°C and the air is still very warm for early September, with the odd storm passing through. Every beach is built up with hundreds of high-rise apartments of a very high standard, and despite the hordes of tourists I get the feeling I'm really going to enjoy this place.

Next morning we awake to find ourselves on a lee shore with our anchor dragging. While getting underway to move to the other side of the bay, the guy on the boat next to us lets his dinghy go by mistake and it drifts into the beach. As we're already underway, we can't help retrieve it. Luckily a local comes down to the beach – but to our amazement he takes off the outboard, deflates the dinghy and puts them in the back of his van before driving off. There's nothing anyone can do; the look on the screaming owner's face is one of pure disbelief. We now have a long wire with a padlock and secure our dinghy everywhere, including to the back of the yacht at night. We also lock the yacht up whenever we leave her, taking special care to check all the hatches. To date, touch wood, we have not had any problems.

The wind is still blowing, so we head around Cabo Cala Figuera to Palma Bay for shelter. On our way we pass the police boat and later learn they are on their way to a luxury yacht washed up on the rocks at Andriano. Happily, the weather is good in Palma so we anchor out and find many natural idyllic bays.

Islote de la Caleta, an island off Las Illetas, only a few kilometres from Palma, looks very much like the place we could stay for the rest of our lives. We anchor in 4 metres of turquoise water and stay four days. We become locals and get invited home for a New Zealand lamb dinner by Wolheim and Jo, a Swiss–New Zealand couple who were swimming around the boat and noticed the flag. Wolheim circumnavigated the

Palma

Las Illetas, Majorca

world in a wooden 75-footer – Jo joined the boat in Sydney to see the world and ended up marrying the owner! They now live in Palma with three children. Also in the bay is a newly opened resort called Virtual, with its own nightclub built into a natural cave. Ian's still going at 2 am in the nightclub, so there's life yet in the old boy. The rest of the days we swim and take the dinghy to explore the small islands, popular with the locals for snorkelling and diving.

We visit Puerto Portels for lunch: it's a marina full of superyachts, cruisers, restaurants, shops and bars. Day and night it's full of beautiful people. Our boat would look pretty small here, and don't dare ask the fees. Grant Carlton, a friend holidaying from England, picks us up and we dine at Flanigans. It's the 'in' place to be seen.

We have booked ahead to get into Club Nautico in Palma, which is unusual, but it's a must-see. We go straight there on the morning of the 14th. Palma, with its five marinas, is always full and a very popular place to winter over. We are put into the king's space (they must've known we were coming), right outside the bar at Club Nautico. Food is a lot more expensive and we're far too close to the bar, but the club is fantastic, there's a swimming pool and gym, and we're only 200 metres from the old town and cathedral. It's also a shopaholic's delight, especially for shoes. Ian goes missing now and then, only to be found at the rubbish dump. Superyachts are refurbished here, and there's super rubbish to be found – I'm so glad we only have so much room. The hardest part is I have to look pleased with every find.

It doesn't take long for word to get around, and suddenly we are surrounded by Aussies who work here. Peter 'Gooch' Tabone and Jim Bell both sailed with us in past years and are now living here. We also meet up with Spike and Vinnie from Doyle Vela Sails. They're ex-boat professionals who came to live here seven years ago and have now cornered the super-yacht sail-making market – they also make us a very handy snuffer for our spinnaker (see tip opposite). Spike told the tale of his versatile 20-year-old Line 7 waterproof jacket. Many years ago he suddenly had to leave his dinner and sail out of port. Not wanting to miss out on dinner, he put it all in his jacket pocket and ate it at sea.

Julian (son of John) Lennon has a restaurant/bar called Red Bar in Puerto Portals Nous and we all decide to check it out, as it boasts an Aussie chef trained by Neil Perry. The highlight of the evening was supposed to be pavlova, but it turns out to be a mere meringue with a dob of cream. We did get to see Julian, though, and the décor was fantastic – Moroccan style with lots of red candles.

Back at Club Nautico, Palma, we catch up with Anna and Murray Thomas and his brother Ian and wife Marie. For Anna's birthday, it's champagne at Abaco at midnight in the old town. It's another Moorish-style venue, with high arched ceilings and unbelievable arrangements of huge fresh flowers, fruit and vegetables (and the prices to go with it).

An old school friend of Ian's from Christchurch, Elizabeth, and her husband, Heinz Oser, fly down from France to join us. We sail out of Palma, already making plans to winter over here sometime. We take the exposed north-west coast as the weather is settled – it can only be attempted in such conditions. With a breeze following, the new snuffer on the spinnaker is given its first run and as Ian does not disappear up the mast, it is deemed to be a success. It is an excellent investment and will make life very easy with the spinnaker now getting more use, even though we still don't see other yachts with spinnakers up.

Reaching Puerto Andratx, I realise why discredited tycoon Christopher Skase lived here and why all the media journalists reporting on his downfall liked this assignment. This small fishing harbour is lined with beautiful traditional homes set among pine trees and rolling hills where everyone gets a sea view. It's nice to be anchoring away from expensive and busy marinas but still in the shelter of a harbour.

Elizabeth and Heinz fly home, and Anna and Murray join us for a day trip up the coast to Puerto de Sóller, where we see some of the most breathtaking water, so deep it is indigo in colour. The scenery is spectacular with high cliffs rising straight out of the sea, and vivid green pine trees on the high mountains behind. Swimming at Peninsula de la Foradada is like taking a dip in an aquarium. We anchor for the night in Puerto de Sóller, the only shelter on the north-west coast, where Anna and Murray are staying in an apartment with a bird's-eye view over the harbour. In typical Anna fashion we celebrate her 50th for the eighth time at breakfast on their balcony, overlooking Spanish terracotta roofs, olive groves, and *Cádiz* lying in the harbour below, all surrounded by mountains.

It's now time to test our two new fold-up bikes and ride 4 kilometres inland to the old town of Sóller. I wasn't sure about getting on a bike again, but after a wobble or two I managed to avoid the old tram that runs from the port to the

Solitary Bay, Cala Murta, Majorca

On the hard, Palma

IAN'S CRUISING NOTES

The Imray pilot books for the local area are fantastic, and when we found a nice sheltered bay, the pilot advised putting a trip line on the anchor due to all the old mooring lines on the bottom. Our yacht had one with a buoy and we duly fitted it. Sure enough, the next day when we lifted the anchor, it came up to within 2 metres of the surface and wouldn't budge. We could see the anchor full of rubbish – it was a fouled mooring. The trip line worked a treat. By taking the weight off the anchor and letting down the chain, we were free.

Palma is a great place to get things fixed, so we hauled the boat out of the water and anti-fouled the bottom. The Beneteau agents here were very helpful. Meanwhile, we had a three-bladed stainless feathering prop fitted that we'd brought from Australia. Unfortunately for the poor Spaniard fitting it, there was an electrical storm and he received a hell of a shock. Luckily for us we had turned off the instruments, something we do during all electrical storms, and there was no damage. The feathering prop gives us greater control in reverse, as the pitch is the same as when we're in forward. It is also very sharp and cuts through any nets or mooring lines that get in the way. Because it feathers back straight, there is a lot less drag in the water when we sail, giving us an extra half knot of speed.

After having difficulty lowering the spinnaker in 30 knots on its first outing, we had a snuffer made in Palma. This is a sock that encloses the spinnaker from top to bottom and allows it to be hoisted without catching the wind, which makes it hard to handle when short-handed. The top of the snuffer is tied to a swivel on which it is hoisted. A continuous line runs from the deck inside the sock to the block at the top and back down to a heavy collar fixed to the bottom of the sock. By pulling on the rope, you raise the collar, gathering the sock and allowing the spinnaker to fill with wind. To take the wind out of the sail, you simply pull the hoop and snuffer back down and then lower the sail at your leisure.

Life's a beach on Majorca

Sun worshippers, Las Illetas

old town. Sóller is a wonderful contrast to Palma. Often the old towns were built inland from the ports to be safe from pirates. Oranges, lemons and olives grow in abundance here and we bought the most delicious local orange marmalade. We still dream of this marmalade and the day we ate the last drop was a bittersweet ceremony.

The inky blue water is beautiful, and just around Cap de Formentor we call into Cala Murta, a bay with a solitary white house. The water is so clear and full of fish life. One thing I couldn't get used to was swimming off the boat for fear of sharks (a fear bred through years in Australia), so I feed the fish bread and judge by the size of the fish whether I swim or not.

Last stop is Cala Formentor, holiday home to the rich and famous, poets and artists. Pine-covered mountains surround this big bay where one cannot anchor, but instead 'pick up moorings'. We are told you have to pay, but we arrive late and leave early – they don't catch us this time.

Breakfast overlooking Sóller, Majorca

IAN'S CRUISING NOTES

Seeing the whole of the Mediterranean's weather pattern helped us plan our trip. The weather systems for the four summer months (June, July, August and September) are quite settled and generally predictable. Each region has its own traditional wind with an ancient name. The mistral (from the Rhône valley in the south of France) is the strongest and can blow in the western Med for up to nine days at more than 50 knots from the north. That's great if you're heading south, but head for good shelter or a port if you aren't moving, or if you're heading north or west. More often than not, the wind is very light with flat seas and 70 per cent of one's time in the Med is spent motoring or motor sailing.

We use two sources of weather reports, which are both reliable. On the Internet we access http://forecast.uoa.gr (note, there's no www.) from the University of Athens. Click on Skip Menu, and follow the boxes on the left-hand side. The top box covers the type of weather you want to know about – we select Winds at 10 m. The bottom box is the time. It forecasts at six-hour intervals for up to three days. It is nicely coloured for wind speed and has arrows for direction. Andrea always watches out for the pink bits, which shows it's blowing 50-plus knots – that's when we don't leave the port.

The other source is RTTY Morse Code on HF radio from Germany, which is transmitted at set times every day. Computer software (which you can download off the Internet) converts it to words and we can see what's happening every six hours, with a range of five days ahead. You can either get the whole of the Med broken down into about eight regions for five days, or the western or eastern Med, again in regions but only for three days ahead.

Where will I find a space? Ciutadella

Minorca

The wind is ideal, so we depart for Minorca and have a great spinnaker run into the port of Ciutadella. What a beautiful old fishing port. If you have a copy of the pilot book of the Balearic Islands, you'll find this port on the cover: we moor exactly where the big yacht in the foreground is lying. Ian spots a space only 1.5 metres wide (*Cádiz* is 4 metres wide) and to the amusement of the restaurateurs and other yachts, we shove our way in backwards. This little exercise gives us the best berth in the harbour at a third of the price of the rolling, exposed Yacht Club option at the entrance.

There are no mountains here; only low cliffs line the coastline, with small inlets leading to small beaches. We bike 5 kilometres inland to the oldest surviving building in Europe, Neveta des Tudons – still standing from the Bronze Age. The old town's narrow interweaving lanes were built to confuse enemies. We love the contrast of colour, from yellow sandstone to all shades of pink. It's a little like going back in time.

Heading south against the wind after two days, we aim for what is called the most idyllic (although windy) bay in the Balearic Islands – Cala Covas. Entering between golden cliffs, the small cove forks into two inlets. We find shelter in one cove, under cliffs that are only metres away, but we are out of the wind and with ropes astern it's very comfortable. As we sail past the cliffs of Cova d'en Xoroi, we see caves in the cliffs

Quaint inlet at Ciutadella

that are now a disco, restaurant and bar – an amazing sight. There is a rough track back over the cliffs to Cova d'en Xoroi, so we set out and walk through fields of stone walls that are unchanged, throwing us back into the last two centuries. Keeping landmarks to find our way back, we pass through traditional handmade wooden gates and swathes of wild rosemary. It's a long but rewarding walk. There are 145 caves in the Cala Covas, dating back to the Bronze Age and later used by the pirates of Turkey while preparing to invade the island in the 14th century. Until only two years ago, people lived in these caves. They've since been evicted to preserve the archaeological treasures of the area.

We explore caves, read and write for a few days – it is such a tranquil setting. The nights are very dark and we are the only ones left in the inlet, but I am spooked by how close the cliffs look and don't dare peek outside. We cannot even see the open sea and go out in the dinghy just to see what the wind is doing. I'd love a dollar for every photo taken of us in the bay, as a lot of tourists walk in here to swim and snorkel.

Our days are spent in huge contrast to each other. Some are spent in cities or towns exploring the history and life as it is today, while on other days we're sailing, visiting bays and swimming, relaxing and enjoying the beauty. In the space of one day you can battle the elements in the morning and by

View from Isabel II Fort, Mahón

dinnertime be dressed up in an exotic town square drinking champagne in style. Tourism is a big part of the Minorcan economy and for cruising it is still a naturally beautiful island; anyone interested in history should visit.

The coastline from Cala Covas to Mahón is picturesque with low cliffs of earthy colours. Mahón has one of the largest natural harbours in the world, and its location has made it a strategic stronghold for nations throughout the centuries. We tie up at the sailing club and provision the boat, as we are told it gets expensive in Sardinia. This is the home of mayonnaise but we fill the cupboards with wine (a steal at €2 a bottle) and the freezer full of meat.

It's getting quiet in the harbour now that October has rolled around. That's nice in a lot of ways, but in another month it will be cold and most places will close down completely for five months. Our bikes come in handy and we visit the village of Trepuco, famed for its Bronze Age talayots (prehistoric megaliths similar to those at Stonehenge). On the other side of a bay called Cala Taulera is La Mola, site of the Isabel II fort and prison where the dictator Franco held and executed his political opponents. It has only recently opened to the public for guided tours, so we front up in our dinghy at 10 am on Sunday, only to find you can only go by car because of the large area it covers. The tour guide, Jackie, is only too pleased to drive us there, so we join a convoy of 40 cars and set off. La Mola only closed in 1969, and many residents of Minorca have memories of relatives who went missing here. We drive past the prisons of numerous modern-day executions. No one goes in there.

Cala Covas, Minorca

Later an Australian tells Ian he's flying the wrong national flag. Red rag to a bull! Ian had gone to great lengths to consult with John Vaughan, a leading Australian vexillologist. John recommended the blue national flag over the traditional red ensign (which can be mistaken for an English flag – and we don't want to be taken for Poms, do we?).

A few days later and it's time to leave. (Ian has chased me around the deck for long enough.) We've been waiting for the right conditions to cross to Sardinia, a 200-mile passage. We go by dinghy into Mahón every day to visit websites for weather updates and to collect messages. The mistral has nearly passed (you look at the weather where you are going, not where you are). Spain has been great, but we're looking forward to another language and a new country.

Trepuco, Minorca

Sardinia and Corsica

October 9, and time for the big crossing. The bay is flat calm at 7.30 am and the forecast looks good, so we decide to poke our nose out the entrance. A 2.5-metre swell welcomes us but we sail on with winds of 15 knots and increasing. By the time it reaches 40 knots, we have to slow the boat down in the big seas. Waves as big as I ever want to see are breaking, filling the cockpit, and one particular wave completely crashes down on top of us. We stop, shudder under the foaming sea, but she is soon sailing again. The boat handles the whole situation under auto-pilot very well and is still surprisingly comfortable. Ian is in his element, sailing single-handed, while I stay below and spot fish through the portholes. On our night crossing the moonlight is helpful, improving visibility. Too much, sometimes: once on my watch I go up to look around, only to see a huge wave bearing down on the boat. I run back below and shut the hatch, too scared to look.

From Minorca to Alghero on the west coast of Sardinia, we cover 200 miles in 25 hours. We're very happy about the performance of the yacht and certainly had a quick trip.

Alghero is fabulous and already we love Italy. We spend a night in the port with its old walled town, cobbled streets, Spanish flavour and great designer shopping, before anchoring in the white-sand bay of Porto Conte. This big, beautiful bay is sheltered in all conditions, and we visit the caves of Neptune's Grotto. It means walking 654 stairs down a cliff face to get to them, but it was worth it.

Among blue skies, sandstone cliffs and very deep seas, we motor up the west coast in no wind and around through the narrow, shallow Fornelli Passage. In the clear water you can see all the rocks – they look closer than they are! Arriving in the fishing village of Stintino, we've notched up our first 1000 miles since leaving Cádiz in August.

Stintino holds an annual regatta of lateen yachts (a traditional fishing vessel of the area) and it's a spectacular sight seeing them lined up on the wharf. At a family-owned restaurant we have delicious spaghetti lobster. A stormy front is approaching our exposed location from the east, so the next morning we sail for shelter at Santa Teresa, 54 miles away on Sardinia's northern tip. From there it's an easy 10-mile sail across the Strait of Bonifacio to Bonifacio in Corsica. We change to the French flag, and spy terraced houses clinging to cliffs. The sheltered inlet of white limestone, towering above the high walled town and the port, is impressive. We are safe now for the big blow that's on the way.

Stormbound in Bonifacio, we are lucky enough to watch the fleet assembling for the around-Corsica race. They try to talk us into entering, but with forecasts of 40 to 50 knots, we decline. Ian is envious and wishes he had his Volvo 60, as the conditions are ideal for it.

Bonifacio is a beautiful historical place, but has a reputation for blowing winds 250 days a year. On Ian's birthday on 14 October, we enjoy a huge bowl of mussels for lunch and fine French food in the evening. We'd forgotten how good French cuisine could be. Our days are spent exploring the old cliff-top village and renting a car to see Corsica by land.

We pass through vast pine forests on this mountainous island; there are granite houses and villages on cliff-faces with narrow roads. The region feels very poor, but we learn the government is buying up most of the land to preserve its historic heritage. We visit Sartène high on the cliff-face, a fishing village called Propriano, the capital Ajaccio on the west coast, and back to Porto-Vecchio on the east coast, our pick of the ports.

Back across the Strait of Bonifacio, we keep a careful eye out for unmarked rocks – they can be lethal around

Cemetery, Bonifacio

Timeless news

Overlooking the port of Bonifacio

Bonifacio

Bonifacio is a beautiful historical place, but has a reputation for blowing winds 250 days a year … Our days are spent exploring the old cliff-top village and renting a car to see Corsica by land.

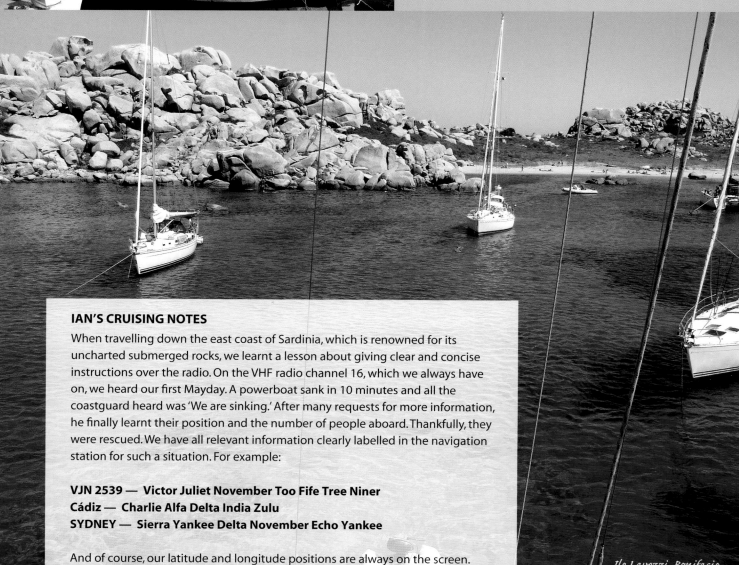

IAN'S CRUISING NOTES

When travelling down the east coast of Sardinia, which is renowned for its uncharted submerged rocks, we learnt a lesson about giving clear and concise instructions over the radio. On the VHF radio channel 16, which we always have on, we heard our first Mayday. A powerboat sank in 10 minutes and all the coastguard heard was 'We are sinking.' After many requests for more information, he finally learnt their position and the number of people aboard. Thankfully, they were rescued. We have all relevant information clearly labelled in the navigation station for such a situation. For example:

VJN 2539 — Victor Juliet November Too Fife Tree Niner
Cádiz — Charlie Alfa Delta India Zulu
SYDNEY — Sierra Yankee Delta November Echo Yankee

And of course, our latitude and longitude positions are always on the screen.

Ile Lavezzi, Bonifacio

Sardinia

here. Porto Cervo, our next stop, is home to some of the world's richest yacht races. We are seeing Porto Cervo as no one else does, as no one is here! Everything is closed for six months. But it's beautiful here, and we would love to come back at race time, if only to see the 600-odd boats leave every day and return at night through a very small entrance.

At the pleasant old city of Olbia, further south, we meet up with our daughter Janey and friend Dara, who arrive by ferry from Rome to stay for a few days. We spend one more day in Olbia with them, enjoying bowls of local mussels and making plans. There's a lot in this area to explore: white beaches with the clearest emerald water, landscapes of pink granite, dotted with impressive holiday homes and gardens. We sail around the Emerald Coast (north Sardinia and south Corsica) for a week, enjoying having Janey and Dara on board. The days are colder now and we have to go to a marina every night to get power to keep warm, so much of the fun has gone.

Sardinia to Italy

Our trip across from Olbia, Sardinia, was another overnight fast trip. As we near the Italian coast, the sea becomes brown and that feeling of 'It's all over for this year' hits us. Entering the marina we surf in on a wave, then do a sharp turn to avoid the beach. Don't blink!

Winter has come with a vengeance, with wind outside now at 40 knots and seas crashing over the breakwater wall. *Cádiz* is now here for the winter. Having taken hundreds of photos and sailed 1500 miles, we shoot our last photo with the camera before it takes to the water and Dara has to go swimming after it.

The day Janey and Dara left, the sun came out and since then we have had beautiful cold, clear days. We spend our days packing up the boat to be stored in a yard up the Fiumicino Canal, going into Rome for the day or just riding our bikes and enjoying the 50 shops and 10 coffee bars on the wharf. We are berthed at a port 20 kilometres outside Rome called Porto Turistico di Roma, at the entrance to the Tiber River. The 1200-berth marina is only three years old, with upmarket nautical fashion shops, restaurants and coffee bars. On the weekend, this is the place to shop and parade in all the latest fashions, from grandma right down to the babies in the latest stroller. What intrigues us is that the clothes are very nautical in style, yet most people have never been on a boat!

This year more than 50 people are living on their yachts over the winter, and they've set up quite a community. Every morning on VHF radio, a volunteer on one of the boats announces all the information for the day – weather, medical assistance, anything for sale and activities for the day. This can go on for an hour, but it is informative and brings people together. Activities are anything from yoga, art, bridge, Italian lessons or talks on different cruising areas, to dinners held from boat to boat and cocktail parties. This is a unique situation in the Med, and great friendships develop. The nationality mix is around 40 per cent English/European, 30 per cent American, and the rest Canadians, New Zealanders and Australians.

Going by train (a very cheap form of transport), we have several days in Rome and love soaking up all the history with not too many tourists around. Rome is a vibrant, living city where pedestrian crossings mean nothing, Vespas are countless, smart cars are in their hundreds, and the aroma of coffee is strong. (They sure know how to make coffee here.)

The yacht has been great throughout our cruise this season. Ian had initially wanted a boat with every mod con: generator, water maker, air-conditioning, satellite phone … you name it, he wanted it. In the end, buying the Beneteau, which had none of these things, turned out to be the right decision. The less you have, the less there is to go wrong, and getting things fixed in the Med is not always easy during the holiday season. Moreover, *Cádiz* is so easy to handle, and has spacious living quarters down below. We have no complaints. Roll on 2004!

I would like to finish this year with a typical Ian quote:
Ian: 'Do you speak English?'
Local: 'No.'
Ian: 'Why not?'

y yacht

CÁDIZ SPECIFICATIONS

Here, for those interested in the technical elements, are the specifications for our yacht, **Cádiz**.

Beneteau Oceanis Clipper 473

Built France 2002
Hull number 169
Construction Hull, solid GRP laminate;
   deck, balsa sandwich
Length overall 14.30 metres (47.3 feet)
Beam (width) 4.31 metres
Draft (depth to bottom of keel) 2.1 metres
Displacement (weight) 11 tonnes
Cabins three, with two heads
Engine 75HP Yanmar
Fuel 240 litres (3.2 litres per hour)
Water 800 litres (four tanks of 200 litres) –
   lasts two people 20 days with generous use

Sails

Area 103 sq metres
Main with lazy jack
Roller-furling genoa
Staysail hanked on inner forestay
Gennacker with snuffer

Electronics

B & G Speed, wind, GPS, depth, etc.
B & G Plotter to operate Maxsea system
   on C-map charts
B & G Autopilot
Furuno Radar
Icon SSB Radio and VHF
Link 20
Laptop connected to GPS, and also to HF radio to
   receive weather fax

Tender 3-metre Zodiac with 5HP 4-stroke Mercury
   (we sling it across the stern of the yacht when sailing)

ROME TO ZADAR

Rome to Capri

We arrive in Rome at the start of April to relaunch *Cádiz* in the Fiumicino Canal. It's cold (only 10°C) but we press on and paint the bottom with the help of our old friend Max Ryan, who has joined us for eight weeks. Wintering *Cádiz* in the canal has worked out well, costing us only €150 a month plus a haul-out charge. The best part was the boat was still there after six months – we're forever alert to the risk of theft, but with the fierce-looking security man and his four dogs, we were sure it would be okay.

The fishing port of Fiumicino has a canal lined with colourful fishing boats but it's dirty, with debris constantly floating past. While the boat is out of the water, we stay in a local hotel with a shower so small that if you drop the soap you can't pick it up. We're able to work on the boat ourselves, which is unusual (usually there are safety and insurance restrictions), but Fulvio the yard owner is helpful. We're glad we removed all the halyards, sails and covers when we hauled her out – they would've been filthy and oily otherwise. As soon as we hit the water and the two drawbridges open, we motor 3 miles down the coast to the city of Ostia's marina, Porto Turistico di Roma.

In the port, life has moved on for all those who lived on board over the winter. It was especially cold and wet, with snow on the decks and dirty oil all over their boats from the Tiber River, but the upsides were the comradeship and the luxurious facilities ashore. I personally couldn't winter over; it would be a very long six months.

Max, whose wife Suzy has just passed away, wants to move on but the weather forecast looks miserable. We compromise and motor south 30 miles, punching into the wind, to Porta Nettuno, a lovely fishing village with a very good marina. It's cold and damp so we sit it out for three days, staying shore-bound every night to get power to keep the heaters on (but it doesn't take much to keep us warm and cosy). Max, who likes to keep on the move, decides to fly to Croatia to visit a friend – he'll rejoin us in Capri.

We love Nettuno, an interesting old walled town and holiday resort for Italians. At a local bar where the owners make their own wine, we perch on stools and drink wine by the glass straight from the barrels with all the old men. We also visit the Second World War American Cemetery, vast and beautifully kept grounds that house graves and a mausoleum built of travertine, a stone rather like limestone or marble. Buried in this peaceful spot are 7861 US soldiers who died in the Monte Cassino campaign in 1944.

It's now mid-April, cold but sunny, and the wind looks good to sail to the island of Ponza. As we leave Nettuno, the water becomes a sparkling crystal blue and we have a great sail. The port of Ponza is a picturesque fishing village with limewashed pastel-coloured buildings and a castle. It's a sleepy island in winter but looks like a very vibrant place in summer, especially for diving. We're a month too early to fully enjoy this place, but would love to come back. We stay the night on the hydrofoil wharf and get moved by the ferry very early next morning – as it turns out they do us a favour, and we have a great sail to the island of Ischia. En route we pass the island of Ventotene, to which the emperor Nero's wife was once banished for being naughty. She was eventually beheaded and given to the mistress. (Better move on in case Ian gets any ideas.)

Ischia port is a delightful but small bay; it was once a lake created by a volcano until the Romans dug a canal to open it to the sea. I can't imagine what it's like in high season, accommodating ferries, hydrofoils, fishing fleets and yachts. In the low season one night costs €50, in high season it's €180 (if you can get a berth). The island is picturesque and famous for its thermal pools, which we'd like to revisit sometime in the summer. We have lunch on the quay, seafood

Under sail to Capri

IAN'S CRUISING NOTES

Every yacht, when travelling to different countries, needs to be a registered ship of a country and have a document that details ownership and country of registry. It is similar to a passport.

Cádiz was a New Zealand-registered ship but we changed her to the Australian registry before we left. Every time you enter a port they ask to sight your papers. This is to check length (for marina fees) and ownership. The marinas supposedly report your presence to the customs authority of the country you are in.

Isola Faraglioni, Capri

Perfect Positano

pasta with a glass of wine, and head back to the boat for siesta time. It's not exactly Med cruising yet, as we're a month too early and it's still very cold and wet.

Our plan for the next six months is to travel along the west coast of Italy to Sicily, Tunisia, Crete, the Greek Islands, Turkey and Croatia. Friends are joining us as we go. I have my Musto 'bear suit' (a fleecy lined one-piece suit) on, and we're sailing south in search of better weather.

Leaving Ischia in the pouring rain, we sail to Capri and out comes the sun. We visited Capri four years earlier and it is still a magic place. Don't just visit with the hordes of day-trippers – stay and enjoy the sophisticated villages, hill-top walks, history and bays. The credit card is out for me and there is a boat show on, so Ian is in his element. We're looking to buy a tender (dinghy), and top of my wish list is *Chocolate*, a brown 40-foot Riva motor cruiser with

white upholstery and lots of chrome. Max rejoins us here and thanks to Ian's negotiating skills, the fisherman next to us gives us a fresh tuna. We circumnavigate the island and motor over to the Amalfi coast only 10 miles away. Positano is magnificent on the approach; the bay is very exposed but the sea is flat calm so we take our chances and moor for a night. Once ashore, we climb the numerous stairs in this carless town and enjoy the colourful and attractive Positano.

We can tell we're the first tourists of the season as the locals are eager to rent us a mooring for the night. They also rip us off ashore – €40 for two beers and a Campari! It's a way of life now, and as we head south we have to be aware of what we're paying. Price also depends on whether you sit down or not, take food on a plate or eat it out of a napkin. It takes Ian hours to get over being taken for a ride and the poor man gets it every time we pass.

Tropea from the boat …

IAN'S CRUISING NOTES

We now have Internet aboard whenever we are in Italy. TIM, a telecommunications provider, offers an unlimited GPRS (General Packet Radio Service) Internet connection (5 pm to 8 am Monday to Friday and all weekend) for €25 per month to its 'pay-as-you-go' mobile customers. By connecting my mobile phone to the laptop, we can send and receive emails, and surf the Internet at relatively fast speeds. We have not found this in any other country but it's fantastic while we're in Italy. The best bit is that you need only sign up for a month at a time, rather than a year.

Tenders (dinghies) are important to have and you need a good-sized outboard. We put a 5HP, four-stroke Mercury engine on a 3.1-metre Zodiac, and she does 15 knots in calm waters with two people on board. To stow the dinghy, davits are great, but we knew from previous experience that they get in the way when mooring. So, in true Aussie fashion, we improvised. Initially, we used our electric halyard winch to lift it onto the foredeck with the outboard still on, but later learned to pull her side-on up the transom, using a block and tackle system (also still with the outboard on).

Tropea from the balcony

RECIPES **ITALY**

MARINATED FRESH SALMON WITH SCRAMBLED EGG

This makes a really special breakfast.

SALMON
½ cup chardonnay vinegar
1 bay leaf
3 black peppercorns, cracked
2 cloves garlic, peeled and finely
    chopped
2 fillets fresh salmon, about 150 g
    each
¼ cup extra virgin olive oil
¼ cup lemon juice
fresh basil to serve

In a small pan, bring vinegar, bay leaf, peppercorns and garlic to a boil and simmer for 5 minutes. Pour over salmon fillets and leave to marinate in the fridge overnight. Next morning, drain fillets, then coat with olive oil and lemon juice. Slice thinly and serve with eggs, garnished with fresh basil.

SCRAMBLED EGGS
3 eggs, lightly beaten
½ cup milk or cream
sea salt and freshly cracked black
    pepper
extra virgin olive oil

In a bowl, combine eggs and milk. Season to taste. In a pan, heat oil and add egg mixture. Reduce heat and let eggs cook slowly, stirring once. Remove from heat when eggs are just set.

MARINATED FRESH ANCHOVY SALAD

1 baby cos lettuce, washed and
    shredded
½ Spanish red onion, peeled
    and chopped
¼ lemon, rind on, sliced finely
25 g capers
100 g marinated fresh anchovies
    (available at most Italian
    supermarkets, not the salted
    tinned version)
extra virgin olive oil

In a salad bowl, combine first 4 ingredients and top with anchovies. Drizzle with olive oil and serve.

VEAL SCHNITZEL WITH CAPER SAUCE

This is just as delicious if you substitute chicken for veal, and/or green capsicums (peppers) for capers.

4 thin veal pieces, each about 100 g
1 egg, lightly beaten
½ cup breadcrumbs, in plastic bag
olive oil for frying

Dip veal pieces in egg, then place in bag with breadcrumbs. Shake until coated. In a pan, heat oil and sauté veal pieces for 2 minutes per side until browned. Transfer to a platter. Pour sauce over veal and serve with boiled parsley potatoes and beans.

SAUCE
juice of ½ lemon
¼ cup extra virgin olive oil
30 g capers

In a small bowl, whisk lemon juice and oil until blended, then add capers.

smoking Stromboli

Capri to Lipari

The Romans were the first to recognise this stretch of coastline as a desirable place to live, where the aristocracy could while their time away in luxury. Cruising leisurely beneath a steep mountain range, we pass mansions clinging to cliffs and small fishing inlets on the 5-mile trip to Amalfi. With such an inaccessible coastline, it's not surprising many claim that the compass was invented here. The ever-present 'man at the wharf' comes out to meet us and the haggling is on again. This is a beautiful area, but don't come in July and August – it must be hell. Our man helps us out later when, 2 miles out to sea, we realise we don't have our dinghy. Very embarrassed, we return for it, knowing the law in Italy says you can keep anything found at sea. We are now well south in search of that better weather, and even the bikini got a brief airing one day. Stopping at various ports for the night in simple old villages, we enjoy visiting the local cafés for a cappuccino, pastry, apéritif or beer with the locals.

In Agropoli we enjoy watching people playing canoe polo between the pontoons: it's an aggressive and serious sport

here. Our last port, Cetraro, looked okay from the water, but has been renamed something unprintable by Ian. The only interesting building was the castle, and that's been left to decay. The numerous old stone villages in the valleys and on hill-tops are being forsaken for newer places on the coast.

Today our crossing of 50 miles is flat calm. The bear suit is off but not much else. Our destination is Tropea, at the top of the shoe's toe, and we're excited about nearing Sicily. Tropea is a delightful old cliff-top town 200 steps directly up from the marina. It's Max's birthday and we can already taste the seafood pasta of clams, scampi and mussels for which Tropea is famous, along with renowned Calabrian produce and wine. We spend time stocking up for our trip to the Aeolian Islands. The Ristorante Tropea Vecchia, which we'd heard about, is exceptional – we have the fresh shellfish pasta and rosé wine.

Leaving Tropea in brilliant sunshine the following morning, we toast a successful stopover with our limoncello, jars of onion marmalade, sundried tomatoes and almond biscuits. It's now the first week of May, and at last the warm weather is here. Our

Dolphins off the bow   Stromboli close-up

cruise to the active volcano island of Stromboli (the so-called 'Lighthouse of the Mediterranean') in the Aeolian Islands is flat calm, but playful dolphins amuse us.

Stromboli is quite majestic. On one side it's life as normal for the locals in their white, flat-roofed houses, set against the deep black rock and black sand. We motor around to the west to see the active side and it's breathtaking. The whole flank from top to water's edge is hot, smoky and noisy. Taking the dinghy in close, we watch pieces break away and cascade into the sea, fizzing and spraying water everywhere. We find out later it's a forbidden area. We spend a night on the island, walking the narrow white lanes and looking for the holiday home of Dolce & Gabbana. It's an exposed anchorage, but with no other options we stay and have an uncomfortable night. Early in the morning, with the wind on the nose, we head for the island of Lipari and its marina.

Lipari, capital of the Aeolian Islands, has been settled since Neolithic times, with a history of endless invasions and eruptions. It's only recently been discovered by tourism, but still has a nice natural feel. Over the past 50 years, more than half the population has left to settle in Melbourne and Sydney, so we are constantly approached by locals who want to tell us of their relations in Australia. It's whitebait season, so we quickly buy some and enjoy New Zealand-style whitebait fritters for an on-board lunch. The Lipari museum is a must-see: pottery, gold jewellery and coins found in terracotta tombs and sunken ships are a wonderful sight. We are fascinated by what looks like a cooking plate, but turns out to be a cock washer. Ian is fascinated and wants one.

For the past few days we've been sailing in tandem with another boat. Tony and Jane have been great company, sharing stories over a wine or two. We all climb to the crater's edge of a volcano on the island of Vulcano to swim in the mud pools and hot bubbling sea water. It sounds all very therapeutic, but it smells like a piggery. As we say farewell, I'm reminded once again that you only see your new friends for a few days, but you become friends for life. We go different ways but will undoubtedly cross paths again.

Cefalù   Sunset, Lipari islets

Sicily

What a welcome to Sicily. With James Pegum and Caryn from London aboard, we leave Vulcano on a brilliant day in sunshine and bikinis ... but how things can change. It's 50 miles to Cefalù and 10 miles out we see a front coming. The pasta lunch and wine glasses on the table are suddenly all whisked away. Shortening sail, it's fast sailing until we see the sea all whipped up like billowing smoke onshore. Then it's down with all sails and harnesses on, bringing a reality check to our guests. We have a policy: you don't look at the wind strength when it gets over 50 knots! Another yacht radios us and wants to follow us in through the entrance. Thankful for our big motor, we slowly enter the bay and anchor in the lee of the cliffs. The waves are washing over the marina and there is no way we can get a berth, so anchoring is our only option. It blows force 10 and *Cádiz* is on her side, but the anchor holds and we wait out the storm that finishes off what Ian and Max, in true Aussie understatement, call 'a fresh breeze in Bass Strait'.

We wake in Cefalù to a brilliant day, swap tall stories with other boats, make more friends and explore the wonderful old village. Cefalù is nestled under a large rocky outcrop, and we quickly fall in love with the village's restaurants, shopping and ice-cream in a brioche. The ever-present narrow cobbled lanes are filled with washing dripping overhead, Fiats zip around, and even the dog deposits on the pavement add to the European atmosphere.

Max hires a car, as this is all too slow for him, and we all travel 100 kilometres inland to Gangi; at the altitude of 1154 metres, I think the snow has only just melted. Getting Ian to leave the boat for one day is a miracle, but he soon forgets and enjoys the country as it's very like New Zealand: very green and about to burst into flower. Medieval stone villages (*un*like New Zealand) perch upon peaks and ridges, and are a wonderful sight. I have read about a 16th-century monastery that serves fantastic Sicilian food, so we venture there. At Gangivecchio we enjoy a set lunch of six courses, including pastries, pasta, risotto, wild roast pork and fig tart, local

Palermo

wine and mandarincello. Our favourite was the pistachio, Gorgonzola and pear risotto.

A charter boat with the Maori name *Hauraki* is in the marina, so the ever-curious Ian investigates and the Polish people on board are only too pleased to find out how to pronounce the name. I still don't know how a charter boat out of Italy, registered in Greece and sailing in Sicilian waters gets a New Zealand name! (Coincidentally, a few nights later during another 50-knot storm – making me start to wonder why we came down here – we hear a mayday and it turns out to be a very well-pronounced *Hauraki*. The rescue boat leaves with its lights flashing dramatically, and later on both vessels return safely. Thanking Ian the next day for the pronunciation, they were soon on their way. It's fantastic that the Italian authorities have the resources to go to the rescue of any boat in difficulties, especially some of the European charterers with little experience.)

Cefalù has been a wonderful stopover for a few days, and with cheap marina fees we are reluctant to leave, but we

need to get to Palermo to rendezvous with friends. Howard and Valmai De Torres are with us for three weeks and Michael and Di Quaife for five days: all friends from Sydney. We've read a few unsavoury reports about what to expect in Palermo: rats, dirt, the Mafia and wantonly dressed women. We're going there to make our own judgment. Additionally, there are said to be two sports there: one is soccer, and the other bag-snatching from Vespas. Hold your over-shoulder bag well away from road traffic, we are warned.

Deciding on the marina right in the old centre is almost not a good idea. It's very crowded and tricky to enter, with mooring lines everywhere. Savoury words fly as we chop a few lines accidentally, but we finally get in. The water is stagnant and smelly, and I can't imagine what it's like in the heat of summer. My skin stings from retrieving the laid lines, but we get to know our new neighbours in the local yacht club and things are looking up.

This is a great time of year to be in Palermo, as it does get very hot later on. It's Sunday and at the end of our dock

In the mountains at Gangi, Sicily

is the Palermo 'Portobello Road'–style antique market. We enjoy the atmosphere with the locals, wandering the marble and stone streets of this historically and architecturally rich city. Ian has tied our valuables around my neck – no Vespa-rider is going to get our things, just my head.

Despite the fearful warnings, we thoroughly enjoy our visit to Palermo. In a wonderful gesture of generosity, a neighbouring yacht gives us organic virgin olive oil from their farm – not one bottle, but a whole case. On our last night here, there are fireworks in the bay. They must know it's my birthday tomorrow.

Three days is long enough to have the boat sitting in stagnant water, and now all our guests are on board, Ian can't wait to get out. We sail west for my birthday dinner to Castellammare, a small fishing village waiting for summer. We wonder at first what on earth is going on: we're greeted by men in army uniforms and peasant women on the dock, people running amok, and shots ringing out. It turns out they're making a movie about the Mafia. We eat at a hit-and-miss restaurant called Mucinera, and it turns out to be one of the best seafood meals we've eaten yet – especially the marinated swordfish, squid antipasto and sun-dried tomato prawns.

We wake to another cloudless mid-May day and motor to Scopello, arguably the most photographed place in Sicily. The water is deep and icy clear, the rocks covered with interesting cacti, and the village on the hill surrounded by wildflowers. In summer people flock here to swim and we can see why, but there's no swimming off our boat today: the water really *is* like ice. The wind gets up, and after an uncomfortable sail we overnight in San Vito lo Capo. Famous for its couscous and Moorish

RECIPES **ITALY**

HONEY NECTARINES

If nectarines are hard to come by, this is equally good with peaches.

2 nectarines, halved and
    pitted but not peeled
3 Tbsp honey
1 tsp ground cinnamon
¼ cup white wine

Preheat oven to 180°C. Place fruit cut side up on oven tray and sprinkle with honey, cinnamon and wine. Bake for 10 minutes. Serve with whipped cream or yogurt.

BANANA, RICOTTA AND HONEY

Fresh Italian ricotta is light and delicious. This breakfast favourite is not only healthy but there's no cooking involved. I don't usually prepare individual servings on the boat, but this calls for an exception.

4 Tbsp ricotta cheese
2 bananas, peeled and
    sliced lengthwise
honey to taste

Divide sliced bananas and cheese between 2 serving plates and drizzle with honey. Serve with slices of toasted Turkish bread.

PISTACHIO, GORGONZOLA AND PEAR RISOTTO

2 Tbsp olive oil
2 spring onions, thinly sliced
¾ cup Arborio or short-grain rice
2 Tbsp dry white wine
2 cups chicken stock, hot
sea salt to taste
20 g pistachio nuts, shelled and
    finely chopped
50 g Gorgonzola cheese
1 pear, peeled and diced

Heat oil and sauté onion and rice for 1 minute. Add wine and stock and, stirring from time to time, simmer for 30 minutes or until liquid is absorbed. Season, remove from heat and stir in nuts, cheese and pear.

town, it's also sleepily waiting for the summer holiday-makers.

Early next morning we head for Trapani; Mike enjoys a spell on the helm and Howard recovers from the couscous (which has produced an unfortunate 'cleansing' effect). We see very few boats on our way. The authorities are trying hard to get more cruising boats to this side of Sicily, but they have a lot to learn about welcoming people. We're faced with pontoons and no facilities for boats at Riviera prices, so most of the time we find a space on the harbour wall free of charge.

Trapani and our following stop, Marsala, are both grand stone cities of palaces, cathedrals, and museums with marble roads and footpaths. We three girls take a bus and visit Erice, a 12th-century stone village high in the mountain with beautifully laid-out medieval lanes and the Castle of Venus. The swirling fog makes it eerie, and it's easy to imagine the history this inaccessible place has seen over the centuries.

Mike and Di leave us and we sail out to the island of Favignana, renowned for its tuna fishing and beautiful turquoise waters. The bays are too shallow for us to stay so we sail on to Marsala, passing the much-photographed bay of Cala Rossa. Another month later and anchoring in these azure waters would be a must, with fascinating caves and coves from the days of quarrying to explore.

On the marina stone wall at Marsala we stay two nights, sampling a few Marsala sweet wines (and some not so sweet). Here we admire a Phoenician ship from 2 BC, found only in 1970 in a nearby bay. Not a lot remains, but what does is displayed very effectively.

Tunisia

With the yellow spinnaker up and a chill in the air that belies the blue sky, we cross to Tunisia. Our plan was to stop over at the island of Pantelleria, but we've set a steady pace and decide to knock off the 80 miles today. Still in search of that Mediterranean summer! Arriving at Kelibia, a port of entry, it takes a tedious two hours to complete the formalities for our visas, but the officers are very friendly. Next morning we are up early to the sound of hundreds of fishermen coming in from overnight fishing and selling their catch.

Tunisia is a fantastic breath of fresh air, alive and colourful. It's nice to get away from the never-ending renovations of Italy and Sicily. Old Italian stone is replaced by white painted Arabian houses and white-sand beaches for miles. At the market, Ian is approached with 'You want a chicken, sir?', as the live bird is held upside down. There's fresh food in abundance, but only what's in season and local. We are soon back at the boat, without the bird but with fresh strawberries and vegetables. The people are so friendly, even to the point of not haggling about the price, which had become extremely tiresome in Italy.

In a local café, the coffee is Tunisian style: strong, black and fantastic. I'm the only woman in the café, which is a bit scary as people can't take their eyes off my blonde hair. The young boys are fascinated that I look so different. I think Howard and Ian are taking offers; I must remember to wear my hat from now on.

We stop to watch fishermen on the back of their boat eating sardines from a makeshift barbecue, and they ask us to join them. We sit on fishing nets and a very dark hand passes us fresh barbecued sardines. They are simply delicious. We leave a bottle of Australian wine, appreciating their generosity.

Once again the winds are kind to us, and we sail 70 miles under spinnaker down the coast to El Kantaoui on the legendary Barbary Coast, home to the pirates of olden times.

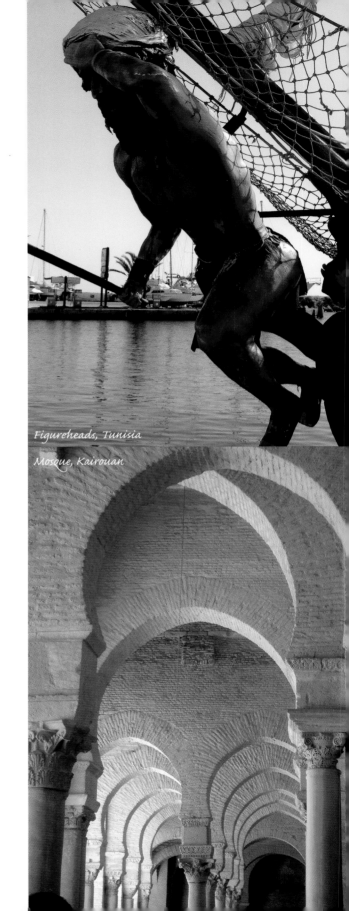

Figureheads, Tunisia

Mosque, Kairouan

El Kantaoui Marina

IAN'S CRUISING NOTES

When departing or entering a new country, you have to report to the local customs post. They always look to see whether the yacht's owner is on board. All countries are paranoid about illegal yacht charters. We expected the formalities in Tunisia to be strict, but there were no issues other than filling in countless forms. Every person on board is required to have a visa, which can be acquired when you arrive. We didn't have Tunisian money or transport into town, so the customs official very kindly went in for us and I paid him back the next day. Customs inspected the yacht and we had to produce an inventory of all electronics, expensive moveable items such as the outboard, and also any alcohol. We were mostly worried about the alcohol, being in an Islamic state, but declared several bottles of spirits and they weren't concerned. Their main interest was mobile phones. At every port the police came to visit but never came on board. When departing, they boarded to make sure we had no extra passengers and that the inventory we had supplied on arrival was all still there. Again, they were particularly interested in mobile phones.

shopping in Kelibia

Thankfully the only pirates are wooden figurines on the tourist pirate ships. We pass beautiful white towns, old and new, with minarets and sandy beaches. After anchoring at Hammamet, we arrive in El Kantaoui, a busy, well-equipped marina surrounded by beautiful all-white buildings (mostly hotels and restaurants). It's tourism at its best and we enjoy a little luxury for three nights, a real contrast to other stops on this year's trip so far. The only problem with this place is that it's 8 kilometres to Sousse to buy supplies.

Arriving in Monastir, we are placed between a Japanese and a German boat, and unwittingly start a battle over whose electricity point is whose. These people have been here for so long that territories are fiercely guarded.

In Monastir a lot of over-wintering boats are still here because the summer is late starting, and now we're holed up here waiting for the wind to change direction so we can head for Malta. Our next stop, 190 miles away, is where friends Nick and Michele Smail from Alice Springs are joining us for a week. Nick is an old school friend, who crewed on a boat of Ian's in New Zealand, and we're all looking forward to the 480-mile sail from Malta to Crete.

With the De Torres we hire a car and make day trips to inland Tunisia. Kairouan is a holy city of Islam, with a magnificent eighth-century mosque, the oldest in Africa. Ian and I wander inside, only to be chased out – we're obviously the wrong religion. Outside the mosque, it's very hot in the narrow maze of white lanes and houses. The Arab summit is on so we travel north to visit Tunis and Carthage, the latter being the Punic city destroyed by the Romans. Flags and flowers line the streets as we pass the Presidential Palace and visit the neighbouring marina, Sid Bi Bou, which seems to be booked out most of the year.

Another day we visit the small village of El Jem, 70 kilometres away, which is surrounded by never-ending neatly spaced rows of olive trees. The highlight is the Coliseum built by the Romans in 238 AD; it's the most impressive amphitheatre in the Arab world and, after its namesake in Rome, one of the best preserved in the world. It's now used for staging operas in the summer, and we explore it thoroughly, even into the lions' den, with very few other tourists around. Our friend Swanny has kept us up to date with the score of the Super 12 final, but right now we are in

Labour is inexpensive here, so we had the boat polished and water-blasted in Monastir.

We visited by taxi a new marina in Hammamet called Jasman. It's a bit more expensive but very clean and professionally run. We would consider leaving the boat in the water here for some time, as it's flushed out every three days. We were very impressed by all the marinas that were being built along all the coasts – they accommodate the boats and also create more villages. If only our coast could have more marinas, we could have a much bigger boating industry, which is a fantastic lifestyle for people and great for tourism. The average marina price in Tunisia is around €15 per night.

Fishermen, Kelibia

our own stadium, only ours has a history of bloodshed and fierce beasts. (Is there any real difference?) Also worth seeing is a museum built around the recently discovered and well-preserved Roman villas with their original mosaic floors (the latter have been spared from the looters over the centuries).

Tunisia is an Islamic state, but unlike a lot of Arab countries, women have distinctly more freedom here. Everyone speaks French as well as Arabic and all the children are educated. The coastal area is certainly more advanced with tourist hotels and evidence of wealth, but inland there are very undeveloped areas and the heat and dust are intense. It's essential to carry your own toilet paper – and develop a strong stomach.

Howard and Valmai leave us and we take a train to Tunis. For lunch I take Ian into an Islamic restaurant – he's not keen, as there is no beer, but I'm determined to have a Tunisian meal. (Ian is looking forward to bacon and eggs in Malta, as pork is nonexistent in this Muslim country.) We have four courses – Tunisian salad, chilli vegetable couscous, fish or chicken with chips, and crème caramel. All for €4 each, and it is delicious. Our best takeaway is a bag of hand-cut chips cooked in olive oil and sprinkled with onion, parsley and small olives for €1. The

boat is starting to smell like a fresh herbs and spices shop, just as it did after we visited Morocco, and again I can't wait to cook with them.

The main purpose of our visit is to see the Bardo Museum, famous for housing the largest collection of Roman mosaics in the world. They are fantastic, telling the centuries-old stories of an illustrious past.

Tunis is dirty, with rubbish everywhere, but the people are well dressed, very happy and friendly. There's no sign of crime either. We pass by the Medina (old walled town) in a taxi, and for our one night in Tunis we find a traditional local restaurant with a live band and atmospheric décor. We soon get into the Arabian music and enjoy watching the locals enjoying themselves.

We didn't know what to expect in Tunisia and have been pleasantly surprised. Yachts are welcomed and the few marinas we've come across are excellent. We believe this undiscovered paradise for yachties will be the next Croatia. Next time we'd love to take a safari trip into the desert and visit the island of Djerba, referred to in brochures as 'the Polynesia of the Med'.

Market, Monastir

Tunisia is a fantastic breath of fresh air, alive and colourful. It's nice to get away from the never-ending renovations of Italy and Sicily. Old Italian stone is replaced by white painted Arabian houses and white-sand beaches for miles. At the market, Ian is approached with 'You want a chicken, sir?', as the live bird is held upside down. There's fresh food in abundance, but only what's in season and local.

RECIPES **TUNISIA**

TUNISIAN SPICED LAMB HOTPOT

A meal in itself, this dish is good with any suitable seasonal vegetable.

2 Tbsp oil
500 g lamb pieces
1 onion, peeled and roughly chopped
1 clove garlic, peeled and sliced
1 tsp ground cumin
1 tsp ground coriander
½ tsp hot chilli flakes
2 cups chicken stock
3 waxy potatoes, cubed
1 broccoli head, cut into small florets
250 g can chickpeas, drained

In a large pan, heat oil and quickly brown lamb pieces. Add onion, garlic, cumin, coriander and chilli and cook for 2–3 minutes, stirring occasionally. Pour in stock, add potatoes and bring to the boil. Simmer gently for 1 hour. Add broccoli and chickpeas 5 minutes before serving.

MUSTARD HONEY CHICKEN WITH CORIANDER SEEDS

1½ Tbsp olive oil
2 boneless skinless chicken breast halves, each halved again
2 Tbsp honey
2 Tbsp whole coriander seeds
2 cloves garlic, peeled and chopped
1 Tbsp Dijon mustard
1 Spanish red onion, peeled and chopped
½ cup cream

Heat oil in a pan. Add chicken pieces, sprinkle with honey and coriander, and sauté for 2–3 minutes each side until cooked through. Transfer to a plate and set aside. Add garlic, mustard and onion to pan and cook for 2 minutes. Return chicken to pan to heat through. Stir in cream. Serve with rice or couscous and green beans.

SPICY CHICKEN WITH AÏOLI

1 tsp ground cumin
1 tsp ground coriander
¼ tsp chilli powder
1 tsp turmeric
2 chicken fillets
30 g butter

Mix spices and place in a plastic bag. Add chicken fillets and shake to coat. Heat butter in a pan, then add chicken. Sauté for 2–3 minutes each side until cooked through. Slice into bite-size pieces. Arrange salad on a platter and top with chicken and aïoli.

SALAD

1 cos lettuce, shredded
½ bunch mint leaves, shredded
2 spring onions, sliced
1 mango or other seasonal stone fruit, pitted and sliced

Gently combine all ingredients in a bowl.

AÏOLI

1 egg yolk
2 cloves garlic, peeled then crushed with a fork
½ tsp curry powder (optional)
½ cup extra virgin olive oil
juice of 1 small lemon

In a small bowl, whisk egg, and add garlic and curry if using. Slowly drizzle in olive oil, whisking continuously until blended with egg. Stir in lemon juice.

Hammamet

Monastir

Kairouan is a holy city of Islam, with a magnificent eighth-century mosque, the oldest in Africa. Ian and I wander inside, only to be chased out – we're obviously the wrong religion. Outside the mosque, it's very hot in the narrow maze of white lanes and houses.

El Jem Coliseum

Bardo Museum, Tunis

Another day we visit the small village of El Jem, 70 kilometres away, which is surrounded by never-ending neatly spaced rows of olive trees. The highlight is the Coliseum built by the Romans in AD 238.

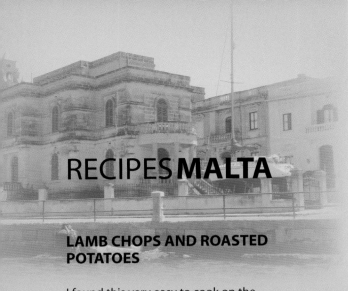

LAMB CHOPS AND ROASTED POTATOES

I found this very easy to cook on the boat as it's all done in the oven.

6 medium potatoes, peeled and
*   halved*
olive oil
4 cloves garlic, peeled and chopped
7 lamb chops
1 tsp sea salt

Preheat oven to 220°C. Place potatoes on oven tray and sprinkle with olive oil and half the garlic. Cook until brown (about 20 minutes), then place lamb chops among potatoes, sprinkle with remaining garlic and sea salt, and cook for another 20 minutes. Serve with mint sauce and green beans.

IAN'S CRUISING NOTES

On our Tunisia to Malta leg, the weather forecasting website forecast.uoa.gr (no www.) was accurate and a fantastic help.

Malta was a pleasant surprise and would be a very good place to leave a boat for the winter; English is spoken there and everything is available for yachts in those nautical shops I love so much.

Malta, Crete and Rhodes

As Doctor Ian ordered, the wind came in from the northwest and on 29 May we set sail for Malta from Monastir. On leaving Tunisia, we are chased and circled by the coastguard. They make contact and all is well. I'm not sure why the customs and police procedures make such a fuss, but we put it down to having something to fill in their day.

Our crossing takes us 190 miles east to Malta in 26 hours. There's one little hiccup along the way when we have no wind and decide to motor ... only to find the engine is not pumping water. One new impeller later (and a very squeamish husband), the wind picks up and we have a very fast trip. Through the night on VHF radio we are intrigued to hear US warships in the area. It feels like we're in a war zone. They closely monitor the speed and position of other 'vessels', as they put it, and if they call you, you may need to identify yourself, alter course or just let them know who you are.

From a distance Malta looks like a concrete jungle, but from inside the double harbour it is very beautiful. And at last it's hot! The first of the world championship offshore powerboat races is being held here, and it's all noise. We are back in the fast lane. We moor alongside beautiful German girls clad in G-strings, and Ian knows he's finally made it.

Nick and Michelle are now on board and we sightsee for a day, visiting Valletta inside the fortified walled harbour. Malta is an island rich in history, so I recommend you see a documentary there called *The Malta Experience*. You'll probably find it screened in the underground chambers, which have over the years been used as ammunition dumps and hospitals. It takes you through fascinating times of sieges, decadence and famine. The mix of different nationalities and architectural styles make this island very interesting. Restaurant Grabiel provides the ultimate seafood dinner, which we finish off with Averma, a cola-tasting after-dinner Maltese liqueur.

Fishing port Mgarr Gozzo, Malta

The next night we anchor in a bay called Blue Lagoon on the island of Comino, and enjoy a great view of the island of Gozo. The lagoon certainly lives up to its name and I may even attempt a swim in the clean turquoise water. We wake to the sound of church bells pealing in the distance.

Crete is 480 miles away, a non-stop trip of three nights and two days. We're looking forward to it very much, especially with four of us on board and Ian predicting an airing for the spinnaker. The plan is to leave late in the afternoon of Thursday 3 June and arrive sometime during daylight on Sunday. We hoist the spinnaker in 15 knots of breeze and settle down for drinks to toast the Maltese islands as they fade into the distance. The sunset is fabulous and we soon start our night watch system: each couple is on deck for two

hours at a time. The spinnaker sock is briefly pulled down but the spinnaker stays hoisted. The wind fills in and out goes the spinnaker – it doesn't come down for two days.

We cross the deepest part of the Med (4300 metres) and it is the most beautiful indigo colour. The nights are bright under the watchful gaze of a full moon. For the whole time we see very few ships and no other yachts, and occupy ourselves with fine dining, wine, good company and old school stories.

At one point, we pass a large drumlike object and decide to circle it. Hanging from it is a very thick rope in 3000 metres of water, and circling it too is a shark. There goes my theory of 'no sharks in the Med'. It's a chilling sight. We see very few dolphins, but one lot sneak up and give us a great show, leaping 3 metres into the air. Then, out on the horizon, we

Leper colony, Spinalonga, Crete

spot a large ship with a huge wake. I comment that it looks like a catamaran built in Tasmania. So Ian makes contact on the VHF radio, and Tim from the US Navy warship replies. The USS *Spearhead* was indeed built by Incat, a company in Hobart. She is big and fast and soon out of sight. The coincidence is amusing – almost no one comes near us on this leg, and when they do we have a connection.

Our guests are getting too comfortable, so with 15 hours still to go the wind changes, whipping up a sea, and we're head on into it. The girls head for their bunks and the boys revel in this crashing and rolling stuff. By morning Crete is in our sights, the winds abate and we serve steak and eggs before entering the port of Khaniá. It's a Venetian seaside town

with lots of character and too many tourists. We tie up to the old sea wall, lined with restaurants looking out onto a stone lighthouse that's still in use.

The weather is now settled and we look forward to finding bays and anchoring out. We sail east along the northern side of Crete and find paradise in a cove called Lautarki: there's one taverna on the beach and we are the only boat. The next bay along is Marathi, a local Cretan fishing resort. We dine on octopus, shrimps, horta (wild greens), stuffed tomatoes and Greek salad. Beautiful white sandy beach, a refreshing swim off the boat; we expect this for the next four months.

It's flat calm so we motor to Rethymno, which the pilot book tells us is the most beautiful port in Crete. A few hours

IAN'S CRUISING NOTES

We finally got customs clearance in Iráklion, Crete, after the two previous ports found it too difficult (or they were just too lazy). After two hours of talking to officials in three different departments, I finally got a transit log – and was pleasantly surprised to find there was no charge. The paperwork must be completed every time you enter a port, taking hours of your time. There has been a big downturn in boats coming to the Greek Islands because of transit fees and paperwork. (Greece, aware that tourism is down, blamed the change on the Euro and then on the 2004 Olympics.) That said, if you read Jimmy Cornell's **World Cruising Handbook** you will find it's actually harder for boaties to enter Australia than Greece.

It was such a relief to have cheap marina fees and set prices, averaging €12 a night, in Greece. We missed the company of other yachts around, but enjoyed Crete, even though it's no longer cheap ashore.

Customs officers also ask to see your current insurance documents. We are insured with Pantaenius, a European company, who specialise in cruising vessels. Their rate is just under 1 per cent. The documents provided are in most languages applicable to the countries we have visited. We've never had a problem with the English version, but did see a Customs official on the island of Rhodes, Greece, asking for a Greek translation from a Frenchman. Eventually the official made him leave to get it translated; not an easy task. When it was my turn, I nervously said I only had English, but he replied 'No problem.' The Frenchman certainly was being very demanding, a policy you can't use in any country.

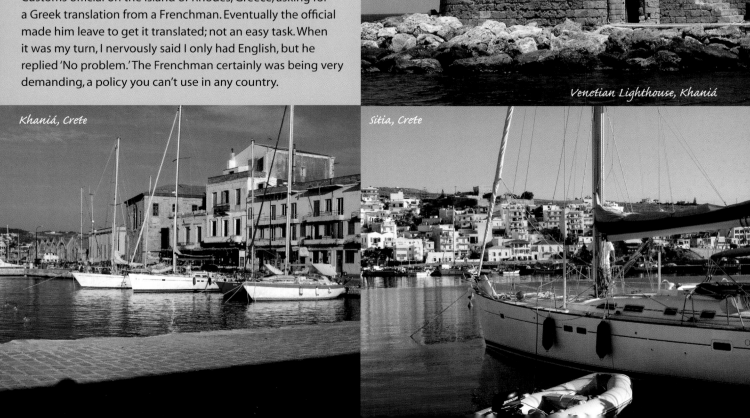

Venetian Lighthouse, Khaniá

Khaniá, Crete

Sitia, Crete

Acropolis overlooking Lindos, Rhodes

is enough and we motor on to Iráklion, the principal port of Crete and, according to the pilot book, not very attractive. We find it an interesting place, and have learned to decide for ourselves rather than solely relying on the pilot book. We find a tight space in the old Venetian port, provision and have some fun courtesy of the nightlife and bars. Here the dress code is 'tighter than tight', so the men find lots to perve at.

Nick and Michelle leave us to return to their camel-tour business in Alice Springs, and Kevin Horne from the CYCA (Cruising Yacht Club of Australia) and *Wild Thing* joins us for 10 days. He's an old crewmember from *Starlight Express* days and can't wait to get out to sea! Eight miles out is an island called Dhia, so we revel in the north-east prevailing winds of 25 knots and sail to this barren dot of land. In fact, the whole of Crete is fairly barren, with a 2500-metre-high mountain range and earthy colours that provide a contrast with the

Mediterranean Sea blues. We share a small inlet with one other Beneteau yacht on its way from England to Cyprus. They call out 'No Aussies allowed!' but we drink their red wine and listen to their tall stories.

Another windy day and we have a great sail to Nossos Spinalonga with its beautiful large, shallow harbour. Wind farms are everywhere now and, to my mind, are an eyesore. It's an uncomfortable night with gusts coming off the mountains down the valleys – the wind farms should have been a warning to us! We now know to give the area a miss next time. En route to Sitia we pass the island of Spinalonga, once a leper colony, where the buildings are still very well preserved. Sitia is small but lively: we find a bar called The Music Room, full of young locals enjoying Cretan food and Cretan rap music. A very memorable night out and well worth the visit. We're getting tired of the locals repeating their sales

View from the Acropolis

Deserted Kasos

pitch to get you into their restaurants, so Ian retorts by trying to sell them his shirt!

Next we go in search of Palm Beach, on the eastern end of Crete. It's the only palm-tree plantation in the Mediterranean, but finding it is like searching for a needle in a haystack. The palms apparently came from Egypt in the 1500s and survived thanks to an underground river. The bay, known locally as Vai, is stunning and reminds us of home; after one day we leave for the Greek island of Karpathos, 55 miles en route for Turkey.

Karpathos is known as the 'windswept island' and consequently gets very few visitors, but today it is flat clam and we motor under brilliant blue skies. Stopping at the unpopulated islet of Kasos, we swim beneath cliffs in water that I can only describe as a magical blue. In the evening we enjoy the local cuisine of stuffed zucchini flower and spinach

pie. Goat is on the menu, but I'll have to pass on that …

Our sail of 58 miles to the island of Rhodes is fast, in a very fresh warm breeze of 30 knots, with Kevin at the helm and loving it. We're soon swimming in the bay of Lindos, with its white Greek village overlooked by a high Acropolis. In the high season it's a very popular holiday resort. Getting Ian to put his foot on the brake and stay for two days is quite hard, but we manage it here as it's so beautiful. We were here 15 years ago with Janey and young Ian, and I recall we climbed to the Acropolis, saying, 'We will have to sail here some day.' We anchor and put a line ashore. It's very hot now, being mid-June, and an early climb is essential before a restful day.

It's interesting to note that the restoration work on the Acropolis undertaken by the Italians in the 1930s already needs to be restored, yet the original structure (built in 200 BC) is still going strong!

Gulf of Fethiye

Cleopatra's Baths

Turkish pancakes, St Nicolas Island

IAN'S CRUISING NOTES

Paperwork on entering Turkey was tedious and four departments had to be visited: cruising permit, health department, customs, visa, and back to customs. It cost around $180. When departing Turkey, it's essential to clear customs, which only means a personal visit to their office to collect stamps. If you don't, you may be refused entry at a later date.

We often 'Med moor' to the shore: this technique involves dropping anchor in 20–30 metres, reversing into shore until you're as close as possible, and tying a stern line to a rock or tree on shore.

Fethiye to the Gulf of 12 Islands

Our 30-mile crossing from Rhodes to Turkey took only half the time we calculated, with the spinnaker up in 20 knots of breeze. Just off the coast, I decide I'd like a photo of *Cádiz* under spinnaker and try an Ian Mainsbridge (Australian marine photographer) manoeuvre from the dinghy. Well, it didn't go to plan, and it's a story I'm not allowed to tell ... suffice to say the spinnaker rearranged itself into four pieces. Lunch is in silence, but all is soon forgotten in a bay of pristine water that's edged with pine trees, especially when we run into some Australian yachties from Newcastle and drink far too much ouzo. Gulettes and yachts fill the bay, all with lines ashore tucked into the pebble beach. Gulettes are traditional Turkish wooden crafts and are used as charter boats. They vary in size, but normally have six double cabins with a crew of three, and at the time of writing cost €280 per person per week, with all food included. Very good value.

Crossing to Fethiye the next morning, we check into customs and survive an exhausting lot of paperwork to obtain our transit log (see opposite page). Kevin leaves us here and we have a few days on our own, so we sail south to Oludeniz (Blue Lagoon). We chartered a yacht here six years ago with friends and had the best time. Wanting to repeat some of the highlights, we moor off the island of Saint Nicolas among 20 gulettes, with New Zealand and Australian flags everywhere. This island has Byzantine ruins dating from AD 330 tucked among the pines, and you actually tie your boat to the ruins.

Oludeniz is a one-stop tourist holiday resort in a dramatic setting, where you can parapont from the 2000-metre mountain down to the beach. It's an exhilarating experience (we did it six years ago) but it can take up to an hour to glide down – a long time to spend away from your boat.

This part of the coast has developed considerably in six years and now has great marinas (and, naturally, the prices to go with it – €40 a night). Gocek marina has the cleanest,

clearest water we've seen, and understandably so, as it's the only place we've come across where you have to use your holding tank instead of discharging waste.

Jane and David Earle from Spain meet us for a week and we head out to the bays. Big decisions have to be made: do we visit Ruin Bay, Tomb Bay, Cleopatra's Baths, Santa Klaus Island, or ancient sites? It's time to relax, enjoy swimming and bay-hopping as the pine trees slide by.

We are very pleased to see some marine life here this time, and even though the fish are small, it's a start. Turkey is trying hard to encourage tourism, with the best brochures we have seen from any country so far. Prices have risen a lot but the service is good and you still get value for money. I like the exchange rate – one million lira equals one Australian dollar – but reality hits when it costs half a million to have a pee! We were told before we got here by fellow cruisers that Greece is now cheaper than Turkey, and they were right.

Leaving the boat at anchor off the island of Delikli, we transfer to an excursion craft to visit the Dalyan Delta. Winding along the river surrounded by bulrushes, we visit the ancient harbour city of Caunos (600 BC), which is now landlocked. High on a cliff face are magnificent tombs carved into the rock for the Carian King and his family in around 400 BC. After a very hot day we head for Ekincik Bay for a swim before dinner.

Since arriving in Turkey, we've sailed a mere 40 miles along the coast – quite a pleasant change from our previous pace. There's so much to see in a small area. The Bay of 12 Islands is off Gocek, surrounded by hills covered in lush green pine trees. A peaceful and beautiful place to cruise, it reminds us of the Bay of Islands in New Zealand. Get over here and charter your own boat. You won't be disappointed. The coastal history and enclosed bays in which to anchor make this area one of the best cruising grounds in the Mediterranean.

Get over here and charter your own boat. The coastal history and enclos bays in which to anchor make this area one of the best cruising ground in the Mediterranean.

Anchor woman, Bozburun

Cherished visitor, Marmaris

Marmaris to Bodrum

As June ends, we spend two nights in port at Marmaris, where Jane and David leave us. It's a hive of boating industry during the day and one big nightclub by night. We will be pleased to get out into a bay for some relief from the noise and heat. To our surprise, we see a lot of Ukrainian boats based here; one is moored next to us and with their perfect English and her perfect G-stringed posterior, they become interesting neighbours.

All the restaurants have big screens showing soccer in full swing, and when that's over the side-by-side nightclubs all compete to play the loudest music. The town is jumping into the early hours, and even in the marina the boat is vibrating.

A turtle has lived in this marina for two years, and we're very privileged to have it come to the boat, feed on some bread and disappear again. Turtles are now an endangered and protected species, so to see one is very special.

Fifteen years ago we chartered a boat and sailed from Bodrum to Marmaris with daughter Janey, son Ian, and Dayne

and Julie Sharpe. We begin the return journey today, recalling fond memories. After leaving Marmaris, we pass the bay of Bozuk Buku, site of an ancient citadel of Hellenistic origin, and remember the kids moaning 'Oh no, not more ruins.'

The wind is filling in and by the time we head into the bay of Ciftlik, it's a full-on meltemi — a hot and dry strong wind, prevailing from the north-west, that can blow for up to five days at a stretch.

We stay the night in Serce Bay, dining in Osmans Taverna at the end of the bay. As you enter these bays, the locals compete to get you to tie up to set buoys or flimsy marinas so you will dine at their restaurants. We don't eat off the boat often, as it's nice enjoying the local produce aboard. Tonight, the restaurant has every flag flying except an Australian one so, as we have done on other such occasions, we leave one.

On the subject of flags, it's fantastic to see all boats in countries such as Turkey proudly flying their national flag, and the same flag also on all buildings and houses. There's

Marmaris village overlooking marina

just the one flag for all occasions, no special marine flag like the Commonwealth countries. We don't see enough flags in Australia or New Zealand, so come on boat owners – get your flag out! (And if you're Australian, that's the blue national flag.)

It's another typical day, with no wind, blue skies, clear blue water, and we're about to take our fourth swim for the day. It's 40°C, with a sea temperature of 26°C – I can't imagine what it's going to be like in July and August. We're now moving up the Gulf of Hisaronu, south of the Datca Peninsula, after spending a night on the wall at Bozburun and one at Keci Buku. Keci Buku, where we anchor under a Byzantine island fortress, is still a safe, perfectly calm bay, but it now has a huge marina on the eastern side. We also revisit the island of Kameriye where, 15 years ago, they were sacrificing a goat and leaving it in the ancient Greek church. I had to return to see if this is still being carried out and, thankfully, it isn't.

En route to Datca we sail into a bay for lunch and are joined by the yacht *Kahurangi* from Auckland, New Zealand; it was the boat to beat back in the '60s, according to Ian. Backing into the old wall at Datca, the meltemi is blowing again. We drop the anchor well out, let it run, go full throttle in reverse, and squeeze in between lots of boats. There's no room for error and our new neighbours aren't amused, but it's another docking well executed. Datca is still an unspoilt Turkish village, offering delicious local cuisine – almonds are fresh, tomatoes are full of flavour, fruit is delicious, feta and yoghurt natural, and the honey to die for.

At the end of the Datca Peninsula stands the ancient city of Knidos, founded 3000 years ago. Floating in the bay, you can dream of an ancient civilisation. On land, you're among the remnants of that era – walking over marble columns and pottery pieces scattered on the ground, up the marble stairs of the amphitheatre, and looking down on the boats in one

Church ruins, Kameriye Island

Knidos

IAN'S CRUISING NOTES

At Marmaris marina you can get anything possible to fit or fix to your boat. It was also very clean and well managed. It took us only 24 hours to purchase some new upholstery for the cockpit and a new sail cover.

of the two bays. Eight thousand people lived here once, and Knidos is famous for its statue of Aphrodite, the first carved nude woman (until then, only nude men were carved). One of the city's most famous sons is the ancient mathematician and astronomer Eudoxos. Still lying in the city's ruins today is a marble sundial he designed and built.

For the past few days we've been following what we thought was a research team complete with a mini submarine. One morning, when they cross our anchor and we try to untangle their mess, we learn they are Australians making a movie for the ABC on underwater archaeology in this area.

Now into the Gulf of Gokova we are at first disappointed by the amount of rubbish thrown into the bays, something we haven't had in other parts of Turkey.

Here the Kiran Mountains are tall and rugged, with craggy bays and tall pine trees. The water is still clear and the cicadas have taken over from the discos, but the wasps move us on a few times. It's a very remote, beautiful area, with not a lot of boats around.

Sailing up the coast of a country with 57 million people, of which 41 per cent live inland, there's no one in sight. We haven't gone very far in the past few weeks, as we love this part of the Turkish coast, and in fact it's our third time here. It's only a blip on the world map and a very small part of Turkey, but well worth exploring. Some 40 miles into the Gulf of Gokova, our destinations are Castle Island and Cleopatra's Beach. The only white sandy beach for miles, Cleopatra's Beach is a unique piece of history. She brought the sand from Africa as a present for Antony, so he could have a beach to sit on. It's quite unusual sand and I can only say it looks like moth eggs. It's well worth a visit, despite the very heavy tourist presence. As for the amphitheatre

Amphitheatre, Knidos

ruins, they date from early Carian times to the Byzantine occupation.

Making our way out of the gulf to Bodrum, we have two beautiful, clear blue anchorages, Akbuk and Kargicik. Both provide good shelter from the persistent meltemi (which is great if it's going in your direction). We spend a happy few days in Bodrum at the first-class marina, enjoy the fabulous Marina Yacht Club at nights and a little retail therapy by day. Marinas are an ideal place for maintenance and Ian is very happy changing oil and filters, and also now very pleased to have his spinnaker back. It's a little smaller, but once again in one piece.

The castle is impressive and houses the largest underwater archaeological museum in the world, with finds from wrecks around the coast along which we have just sailed, dating from the Bronze Age to the Ottoman period. The ships were amazingly advanced for their time, and in fact anchor designs have only changed in the last 100 years. Bodrum is also the site of one of the seven ancient wonders of the world, the Tomb of King Mausolos from 377 BC. Sadly, only the foundations remain.

The atmosphere at Bodrum is great and it would be easy to spend a long period here. Once again we're surprised to see large numbers of charter yachts and gulettes not being used. Where are all the tourists going?

Coincidences seem to keep happening to us, and today on another yacht refuelling was Eddy, the Musto agent from Germany. He charters a yacht in Turkey every year and believes it's the best cruising spot in the Mediterranean.

We leave Turkey with fond memories of beautiful bays, translucent water, clear skies, warm winds, antiquities, wonderful foods, and lovely honest people. We will be back.

RECIPES **TURKEY**

MINCE PATTIES WITH CHUNKY TOMATO SALSA AND TZATZIKI

In Turkey, mince is made from lamb and can usually be bought in ready-made patties. It is set off to perfection by the piquant salsa and cooling tzatziki.

CHUNKY TOMATO SALSA

2 Tbsp olive oil
1 clove garlic, peeled and finely chopped
1 onion, peeled and cut into 2 cm dice
1 small red chilli, finely chopped (optional)
2 tomatoes, unpeeled, cut into 2 cm dice
1 each yellow, red and green bull horn peppers, deseeded and cut into 2 cm dice

In a pan, heat oil and cook garlic, onion and chopped chilli if using until brown. Add tomatoes and diced peppers and cook over a medium heat for 15 minutes, stirring frequently.

TZATZIKI

1½ cups natural yogurt
1 small Lebanese cucumber, peeled and finely diced
1 clove garlic, peeled and finely chopped
2 Tbsp lemon juice
1 Tbsp chopped fresh mint or 1 tsp dried

Combine all ingredients in a bowl and refrigerate.

PATTIES

500 g minced lamb
2 Tbsp dried oregano
sea salt to taste
extra virgin olive oil

With wet hands, shape the mince into a log. Cut into circular patties. Sprinkle with dried oregano and salt. Heat oil in pan and sauté patties until cooked (time varies according to thickness of patty). Serve patties topped with warm salsa and tzatziki.

PORK CHOPS WITH ORANGE AND CUMIN SEEDS

olive oil for frying
4 pork chops
1 Tbsp butter
1 clove garlic, peeled and chopped
juice and thinly sliced rind of 2 oranges
1 Tbsp brown sugar
2 tsp whole cumin seeds

In a pan, heat oil and sauté pork chops. When nearly cooked, add butter, garlic, orange juice and rind, brown sugar and cumin seeds. Simmer for a few minutes to reduce sauce. Serve with green vegetables.

Bodrum

IAN'S CRUISING NOTES

Greece is stricter than other EU countries on paperwork. It demands that every yacht entering purchase a cruising permit, even EU-registered ships. The cost is €40, although some yachts have been charged more. You have to visit several 'government' departments, a time-consuming process, and they will only issue you a permit valid for six months at a time. Also, if you leave Greek waters and then re-enter, you have to start again with a new permit. At every port they want to stamp and sign the permit as you arrive and leave.

Ios

Santorini

Kos to Naxos, Greece

As we leave Turkey for Greece we have to obtain a new permit (see opposite page). It is only 12 miles to the Greek island of Kos, where we meet our daughter Janey. Our plan is to sail south with her to the islands of Amorgos, Santorini, Ios and Paros.

Once you get past the fast food and loud music, Kos is interesting. History is strewn everywhere, in the form of Roman mosaic floors and painted walls. Our evenings are spent listening to roots and blues music while sitting under bougainvillea and pink oleander in full bloom.

Our next island is Kalymnos, where the blue water and whitewashed houses make up for the barren terrain. Our first meal ashore, in the bay of Emborios, is superb local chicken.

A day's motoring into the wind takes us past islets amid larger islands misshapen by earthquakes. We're heading for Amorgos, where they shot the movie *The Big Blue*. Stone walls creep like veins up the bare mountains and crisscross to form paddocks; they are 2000 years old and the area was cultivated once, but nothing grows here now, not even an olive tree: the soil has long been blown away.

The port of Ay Annas is small and as rustic as it gets, with every house white with blue trimmings. Out to the bay of Ormos Kalotiri and Ian is looking for Shirley Valentine. These are very lazy days in the hot sun. We swim and move on. In Katapola, we learn it's the 41st Aegean Rally, an island race out of Athens. We're invited to the prizegiving, where we sample the local speciality of lobster spaghetti. Unforgettable!

The highlight of this island is undoubtedly the visit to a ninth-century monastery high in the mountains. We climb 300 stairs and don enough clothes to hide every inch of skin. Inside, where three monks still live, we are welcomed to sit down at their table and sample sweets and local liquor. The monastery clings precariously to a cliff face and houses an icon that was found in the sea below the cliff.

Santorini, our next island stop, is amazing: it's one vast volcanic crater. Rumour has it that the lost city of Atlantis is hereabouts. The anchorage at Thira is not ideal, but we take the risk on this perfect day in 50 metres of water. On our entrance there are daytime fireworks, and we learned later that the Olympic torch relay had just passed though.

The cable car takes us up to Thira town and we bus to picturesque Finikia. The views from the summit ridge are spectacular and make up for the crowds of tourists. Everyone should see this place! The island in the middle of the harbour is essentially a huge pile of black coal, and the plug for the volcano that locals say could blow at any time.

The island of Ios gets my vote for great sandy beaches. It's said to be the nudist island, and ... where is Ian? I finally find him wandering the bays, and also meet lots of young New Zealanders and Australians working here for the summer. It's great watching the Bledisloe Cup live in the local sports bar with them. The wind keeps us in port, but after two days we have seen the island on motorbikes, eaten at the Octopus Tree Café (with octopus hanging in the tree to dry), and sunbathed on the beach, which Ian never does. It's time to move.

The wind is lighter around 5 am according to the local fisherman, so we're up early and travel 20 miles to our next island – Paros. We make for the sheltered bay of Alyki on the southern end. Paros has some of the best golden-sand beaches around and is famous for its white marble. I am fascinated by all the marble: they build everything with it, including fence walls and the breakwater at Pisso Livadi marina.

Another early start and we dash across to Naxos for a little land therapy. Back on the windy coast, we're berthed in the port right on the promenade. We enjoy the waterfront of the main town, Chora, and could have stayed longer, but weather information on the Internet predicts we have one more average day before it's really going to blow.

Mykonos, meltemi blowing

Mykonos to Athens

Our destination is Mykonos and the wind is on the nose. For 10 days the meltemi's been blowing a steady northwesterly up to 40 knots. Most boats stay in port but oh no, not us! The lone sailor Ian gets us through (Janey and I are hiding in our bunks). The wind keeps us from reaching the main town on the northern side. Approaching Ormos Ornos, we cheekily slip among some powerboats anchored stern to in a cove, and find great shelter. Despite the high wind, we're loving the cloudless weather. The boat sits in clear blue water and the superyacht paid hands don't mind keeping an eye on *Cádiz* as we explore the island while the wind settles down.

Mykonos is a place for the rich and famous, straight or gay, all having a great holiday, and we relish our few days here. There is nothing to do except sunbathe and party at Super Paradise beach, then dress up for the evening parade in the old town, which starts at around midnight. At 2 am it's disco time at Space (entry charge €30) or Cavo Paradiso

(€55). At Bar Uno we chatted to Greek-Australian actor Nick Giannopoulos (from *The Wog Boy*) who visits every year.

Twenty miles west, we ready ourselves for a little more culture in Syros, the capital of the Cyclades. Tonight in the town square only 100 metres from the yacht there's a live Greek concert. With a line-up of 10 mandolins and eight singers, it's a fabulous show. Janey leaves us on the fast ferry the next morning at 4 am, so it's just as well we stay in the port and don't have far to walk.

The late July weather goes from the sublime to the ridiculous for the last of our Cycladic Island visits: no wind, and a sea like glass. From Syros we head to Kythnos and then Hydra, an island south-west of Athens. The New Zealander in me is happy to see trees as we approach the mainland (the Cyclades were very barren). Hydra is quaint but busy: for the first time we are second row out from the breakwater, and by 8 pm yachts are four rows deep, all stern

Moored four-deep at Hydra

to bow like a puzzle. This is the only town at the head of the bay, where horses and donkeys replace cars or bikes.

Next port of call is Poros, an island with only 200 metres separating it from the mainland and a very pretty entrance in shallow water. Hydra and Poros, with their good ports, had a great naval fleet and were the backbone of the Greek war of independence against the Turks in the 1820s.

Methena translates as 'stinky town' because of the hot mineral sulphur water that bubbles out in the harbour. It's too hot for thermal swimming, but we take the boat in anyway – the pilot book reports that the sulphur eats the weed from hulls – and then leave. Our last taste of crystal-clear water for the moment is on Aegina in the bay of Perdika.

Athens, or should I say the new Athens, from the water is a magical sight. Olympic venues line the coast with the Acropolis in the background. And there's no pollution! I can't believe we have no trouble getting into a marina right next to the Olympic yachting venue at reasonable prices. The Alimos marina at Kalamaki is on the new tram line and only 5 kilometres from the centre. We love being so close to all the action, with excellent shopping and chandleries for Ian.

Mike Fletcher and Dayne Sharp (Australian Olympic coaches) come down to see us and it's great to see familiar faces and swap stories. On Sunday we catch the tram and head for Marina Zea, the Mounikhias marina (home of the Royal Hellenic Yacht Club with great restaurants and bars), and of course the Acropolis. All in all, Athens looks fantastic. Glifadha is a trendy area on the tram line, with modern restaurants and shops. Kitchen Bar was our favourite nightspot, and it's within walking distance of the marina.

The mercury reaches 35–40°C every day now, with relentless blue skies. We run into more Olympians from both Australia and New Zealand, and enjoy hosting them on *Cádiz*. We could be tempted to stay, but we have a regatta to join in Croatia and have to keep moving.

Delphi ruins, high in the mountains

Inside the castle walls, Navpaktos

IAN'S CRUISING NOTES

Traffic under the Rio-Antirrio bridge, at the western end of the Gulf of Corinth, is closely monitored. From 7 miles out, we must make contact with bridge control and follow their directions. When we are 7 miles away, we must radio to let them know we have left.

Before we left Patras, we topped up our diesel from the truck on the dock. I think some have dodgy gauges, as our usage leapt from 3.5 litres an hour to 5.6 litres. Watch your usage here: cruising in the Med typically requires 60 per cent motoring.

Corinth Canal

Salamis Island to Andrea Bay, Greece

Leaving Athens on an afternoon breeze, we head for Salamis Island to prepare to pass through the Corinth Canal the next morning. This canal is 5.6 kilometres long, 20 metres wide, 250 metres high, and 8 metres deep. And consequently it only runs one way at a time. It's a shortcut to the Ionian Islands between the Peloponnisos Peninsula and mainland Greece, cut through beautiful white limestone that gives the water a teal colour. We chance upon the perfect day to go through, as the wind can funnel through here and build up a strong current. The canal is renowned as the most expensive pass in the world (for its length), but to us the awe-inspiring experience and saving in extra miles we would've otherwise travelled was well worth the €190 fee.

Gliding out into the Gulf of Corinth, there's no wind at all. The sea looks like a mirage and we motor all day in the heat. One of the pleasures on a day like this is being able to curl up in a corner and read. We are almost 'ruined out', but we must visit the Delphi ruins near the small port of Galaxidhi, 30 miles away. As we tie to the wall, suddenly music starts playing, horns blow and police car sirens go off. After a startled look around, we spy the Olympic torch coming down the road. It's great to see the whole town out, flying flags and dressed for the occasion. Only the day before, the flame was in Delphi, where the Pythrian Games in honour of Apollo were held every four years, thousands of years ago in the stadium that still stands today.

The marina at Itea is closer to Delphi, so we head there the next day and bus 30 miles through a valley green with olive trees and up the mountain. Terraced into the rock face is Delphi, the geographical centre of the world for the ancient Greeks. The Temple of Apollo is being restored and the theatre and stadium are quite spectacular, but be prepared, it's quite a climb up over polished marble steps to reach them. I'm also fascinated by the concrete aqueduct that transports water beside the road. It's 3 metres wide and takes rainwater from the top of the mountain and down to the valleys below to service their needs.

The next port, Navpaktos, more than lives up to our high expectations. We enter a tiny, pretty harbour between Venetian castle walls. Even with barely enough room to drop anchor and the night-time noise from numerous bars around the castle walls, we are charmed enough to stay.

Generally we've been unimpressed by Greek food. The restaurants seem to offer the same dishes everywhere; Mama cooks in the morning and it's reheated in the evening to serve. It's a real treat when you find a good eatery and we're lucky here. Navpaktos, with its trendy restaurants and bars, is the home of Maria Loi, who specialises in ancient Greek cooking. She has a TV show and wrote a recipe book for the Olympics that hit number five on the best-seller list in Greece. At her establishment on the quay, named Koyzina, we feast on stuffed zucchini flowers, aubergine moussaka and fresh grilled fish. It's so good we have both lunch and dinner there.

From here we can see the impressive new Rio-Antirrio suspension bridge, which crosses the 1-mile strait at the western end of the Gulf of Corinth. It's fun to spot the many superyachts and powerboats obviously heading for Athens and the Olympics, and as we leave Navpaktos we hear *Spada*, owned by New Zealander Peter Cornes, calling up the bridge's traffic control.

We make a brief stop in Patras, the third largest city of Greece, to meet up with Colin and Tammy Selwood from Sydney. The marina is so smelly it burns my nose, and the charges are higher than Athens. We quickly motor to the Ionian island of Cephalonia 50 miles away. With night drawing in we stop at Andrea Bay (of course) at the southern end of the island of Ithaca, the home of Homer's Odysseus. Oh what joy to be back in beautiful clean water!

Cephalonia, Greece to Brindisi, Italy

The Ionian Islands are clearly a favourite with everyone: superyachts to small sail craft, huge powerboats to day cruisers. Cypress, olive and pine trees cover the islands, and amid clear water we spend perfect nights anchoring in bays. It's early August, school holidays and high season for tourism. We lazily motor from island to nearby island in the hazy heat.

Friskardho on Cephalonia is the St Tropez of Greece (so they say), and it certainly was fabulous. We've never seen so many boats all in one bay, by a tiny quaint village. It's more amusing just sitting in the cockpit and watching all the goings-on, although we do venture ashore to join the dining frenzy on the waterfront. Most of the villages around have lost their character due to numerous earthquakes, and this is the only village that hasn't been affected.

The Stenon Meganisiou passage between the islands of Levkas and Meganisi is as picture-perfect as the pilot book states. Meganisi is shaped like a hand with five fingers: the inlets hold deep turquoise water, are fringed by pebbled beaches, and are visited only by yachties. Unfortunately, a lot of yachties now know about it – we're anchoring stern to again and there are boats everywhere.

Now for the place guaranteed to induce envy – we pass by Skorpios, once owned by Aristotle Onassis and a favourite spot of the late Jackie Kennedy. In its heyday it was a holiday destination for the extremely wealthy and a paparazzi hot spot. Skorpios is still privately owned, beautifully manicured and quite stunning. You can anchor off the port or beaches, but you cannot set foot on the island. In my next life I'm coming back as a cicada: they have free rein over this perfectly planted paradise. Two hundred staff work on the island, now only visited for one week a year by Onassis's granddaughter, Athena.

In Levkas, once part of the mainland and now an island, we pass through the Roman-built canal to the main port and then through the bridge (it's actually a barge they pull to one side on the hour). Levkas town is a great place to re-stock and apparently a cheap place to winter a yacht out of the water – but then we heard about the frequent earthquakes and yachts falling off cradles. No, thank you.

Approaching the tiny island of Antipaxos, the 'Maldives of the Med', we see a mass of boats in Emerald Bay, their hulls glowing blue from the reflection of the pure white sand on the bed. It's like sitting in a glass of water. Ian and Colin want front-row position to observe the glamour all around, including the glamour floating on colourful plastic Lilos wearing the skimpiest of bikinis. Then the wind changes, boats get a little close, there's a touch of tension in the air, and the Treleavens have a moment (of course, it's my fault).

We up anchor and head for the port of Gaios, the main town on the island of Paxos, and find a very pretty inlet lined wall to wall with boats. It's sheltered, but we don't need it as there's no wind. Again. Paxos is famous for its olive oil; Harrods of London buy their stocks from here. It's been great having Colin, a chef in Sydney, on board, and together we have reinvented Greek cuisine. Try feta-stuffed green horn peppers (see page 95) and stuffed tomatoes with herbs, all cooked with lashings of the very best Paxos olive oil. Mmmm. One of the smallest islands in the Ionian group, Paxos is becoming a holiday retreat for the rich and famous. Some have their July holiday house here and their August holiday house in Porto Cervo, Sardinia.

Corfu and its many occupying influences make this a fascinating town, built on a promontory between two fortresses. French and Italian architecture coexist alongside an English cricket ground, and it's all within walking distance of our boat in the marina NOAK. One night we attend open-air opera in the old Venetian fort, featuring contemporary traditional Greek singing supported by the Corfu Orchestra.

Friskardho, Cephalonia

The Olympics are in full flight and we watch the opening ceremony on the big screen in a bar, not understanding a word. Saturday night is amazing – there are crowds everywhere late into the night, and the bar by the marina is still in full flight at 5 am.

Colin and Tammy leave us here and we spend a day on boat maintenance before our son Ian and his friend Karina join us for a week. Having been so impressed with Paxos and Antipaxos, we sail back to spend several days there with young Ian. Emerald Bay delivers the goods again, as we swim, dive and enjoy the amazing colours. Weather is an important factor and our timing here is perfect (it's just after mid-August), but Paxos and Antipaxos are also our favourite places in Greece. I can still taste the local orange honey marmalade and olive oil – too good to be true at €7 a bottle.

Corfu is our hop-off point for Croatia, and we plan to go via Brindisi, Italy, to drop off young Ian to catch a train. Motoring all the way on glass-like seas, we stop for a night on the island of Erikoussa 30 miles north of Corfu.

It's an early start the next day, and we're in pitch-darkness as we start the 80-mile motor to Brindisi on the east coast of Italy's boot. Brindisi is primarily a transit ferry town for the Adriatic, but we are pleasantly surprised and enjoy being back in Italy. The pilot book says to lock everything to the deck, which we do, and have no problems, thoroughly enjoying our free stay on the wall.

We have a Sunday to explore the province of Puglia, which is flat, very fertile and famous for its produce, wine and cooking. Hiring a car (clearly Ian has missed driving), we zip at 130 kilometres an hour down the highway to Lecce, known as the Florence of the South. The numerous elaborate churches and cathedrals look like wedding cakes, but it's Sunday and the place is deserted. I'd like to spend more time here and explore the narrow marble streets, eat at the local restaurants and shop at all the designer shops, but they're now closed. Well planned by Ian. What is open, happily, is the famous Café Alvino. Its *granita di caffe* – slushy frozen espresso topped with lashings of cream – is simply delightful.

Off we go again through country lanes surrounded by vineyards and olive groves. Our next destination, the old but pretty town of Oria, has an elaborate painted domed cathedral and a castle. The day's highlight is lunch at Fuori Porta, at the stone-arched entrance to the town. Our order of antipasto comes on 10 plates, all very fresh, delicious and very Italian. And just when we're thinking that's it, along come the mussels, scampi and fresh cherry tomato pasta, washed down with one of the renowned local rosé wines. It's a gastronomical feast.

Ostuni, locally called the 'bright white town' for its whitewashed houses, sits atop a hill overlooking flat green fields to the blue Adriatic Sea in the distance. Around this area are the unique Trulli buildings, built from stone and painted white in a style best described as 'upside-down icecream cone'. Who knows when they were built and for what purpose. They are now used for houses, and every room has a cone.

The day's final mission is to hunt down local caves that contain 1000-year-old religious paintings. Even though the brochures tell us they are here, it's a navigational nightmare trying to find them. On a back road in the middle of nowhere we finally find Cripta di Biagio, a cave on the side of a small hill, and it is truly amazing. Small communities lived here in the caves and only the church was painted, painstakingly depicting the story of the Bible.

An exhausting day, but well worth it and of course the car is full of wine. We finish off with a fantastic pizza in the Windsurf Pizza Bar opposite the boat on the wharf. Translations into English create a few laughs: Gorgonzola pizza has become gynaecologist pizza! They say southern Italy is the poorer part, and we did find this to be true on the west coast; but on the east coast, where only local tourists seem to visit, it certainly isn't, and we will be back.

IAN'S CRUISING NOTES

Corfu had great nautical shops, the cheapest we'd encountered yet, and it's another very good place to winter your boat. The local market was also cheap and accessible. Leaving for Croatia, we were told to avoid Albania or stay two miles out from the coast, for fear of pirates. As young Ian had a train to catch in Brindisi, Italy, it took us only 30 miles out of our way to cross to Italy and was a safer way to go.

Corfu

Fishing boat with outhouse

Market, Corfu

Emerald Bay, Antipaxos

RECIPES **GREECE**

FETA-STUFFED TOMATOES

It's hard to beat this combination of sun-ripened tomatoes and tangy cheese. Good served hot or cold.

2 large tomatoes
50 g feta cheese
1 clove garlic, peeled and crushed
2 tsp chopped fresh oregano
olive oil

Preheat oven to 180°C. Slice tops from tomatoes and scoop contents into a bowl. Reserve tomato shells. Chop tomato flesh, and drain liquid (don't throw it away: add to your next pasta sauce). Drain tomato pulp and mix with feta, garlic and oregano. Pack mixture inside tomato shells and place on oven tray. Drizzle with oil and bake for 20 minutes.

FETA-STUFFED GREEN HORN PEPPERS

These are simple and make a delicious lunch, either as a side dish or for a main course.

50 g feta cheese
2 tsp dried mint
2 green horn peppers, sliced in half lengthwise
  and deseeded
olive oil

Preheat oven to 180°C. In a bowl, combine feta and mint, using a fork to mix well. Stuff pepper halves with feta mixture and place on oven tray. Drizzle with oil and bake for 20 minutes.

RECIPES **CROATIA**

TRUFFLE RISOTTO

Truffle paste and fresh truffles (in season) can be found in most southern European countries.

1 Tbsp olive oil
2 spring onions/shallots, peeled and thinly sliced
2 cloves garlic, peeled and finely chopped
¾ cup Arborio or short grain rice
½ cup dry white wine
2 cups hot chicken stock
1 x 100 g jar truffle paste (can be bought in
  Croatia)
sea salt
1 small fresh truffle, grated
50 g Parmigiano Reggiano cheese, grated

Heat oil in pan and sauté spring onions with garlic and rice for 1 minute. Gradually add wine and stock 1 ladleful at a time until absorbed. Remove pan from heat and stir in truffle paste. Add salt to taste. Serve with grated truffle and cheese sprinkled on top.

Dubrovnik

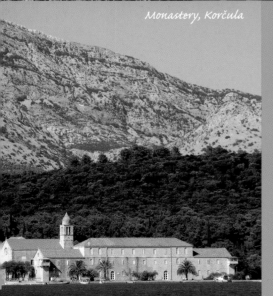

Monastery, Korčula

IAN'S CRUISING NOTES

Upon arriving in Croatia, before going to a marina it's compulsory to land at the Customs dock and visit the office. They issue a cruising permit for one year and you can leave and re-enter Croatia as many times as you like on that permit (unlike Greece). Their main concerns are that you are the owner-operator and are not engaging in commercial work. The permit is inspected by staff at each marina. Before finally departing Croatia a proper clearance is mandatory. A cruising permit costs €235 for 12 months, with no restrictions on leaving Croatia and returning.

Dubrovnik to Kornati Islands, Croatia

Always leave the best until last. Young Ian and Karina take the train to Venice and we sail out in headwinds, making a 130-mile crossing to Dubrovnik on our own. The walled city is very grand, with a small fishing port now closed to yachts. The mix of the old walled town and the new stone houses with their uniform orange roofs, all surrounded by pine trees and a rocky waterfront, is magical. This place was at war only a few years ago and was badly damaged, but with international aid they have restored it to its original glory.

Tying up at the main port marina we walk the medieval fortress wall that encloses Dubrovnik, with no traffic other than pedestrians. A lunch of steamed mussels, squid-ink risotto and fried squid rings in one of the many squares is excellent (though we soon find that the menus in Croatia hardly vary, which is a little dull). Elizabeth and Heinz Oser from France join us today for 10 days and we plan to sail our way up to Split, passing by the many islands.

The local market is on our doorstep in the main marina: the produce is fresh, cheap and seasonal. An old lady from the mountain village sells her goat's cheese, olive oil and herb vinegar. Just watch out for the young man selling fresh strawberries that are great on top but rotten on the bottom.

A storm builds as we head out to the green island of Mljet. When it breaks, the rain is a welcome relief, and the next morning it's another blue day as we skirt the shores of the island to Luka Polače inlet. The pine trees and many rocky bays make it a favourite with the large cruise boats; when night comes, on go their lights and the bay becomes a fairyland. Another highlight is when the local fisherman comes alongside and sells us fresh crayfish, which Heinz cooked to perfection. The salt-water lake, with its monastery set on an island in the middle, is worth a visit.

On the island of Korčula the city of the same name is probably the best-preserved medieval settlement in the Mediterranean. It held a strategic position in the Adriatic over the centuries, where its tall towers could monitor the passing galleys and sailing ships. It's also the birthplace of Marco Polo, whose restored home is worth a visit.

Sailing past the coastal cliffs of the island of Hvar, patchwork colours made by villagers farming lavender, sage, rosemary, olives and grapes are a beautiful sight. From the sea, Hvar shows off its wonderful promenade with a row of palm trees, the Venetian settlement, and an old walled fortress watching from overhead. But one night in this crowded bay is enough, and we happily move on.

We go in search of a beach I remember seeing years ago on a Croatian poster, and find it not far from Hvar on the island of Brač. It's a perfect day and we swim ashore, but the sand turns out to be big white pebbles. We overnight in Lucice on Brač, a remote bay where you pick up a mooring and pay for the privilege – but they do deliver fresh bread for breakfast.

If you visit the nearby island of Žirje, watch your step: there are still unexploded mines around, relics of the recent conflict. We do stay overnight, but Heinz treads very gingerly while attaching the stern line ashore.

Our next stop, the Kornati Islands, comprises a national park 150 miles north of Dubrovnik, established to encourage marine life. The park resembles a lunar landscape – it's 36 kilometres long and 6 kilometres wide, encompassing 147 barren, cone-shaped islands set against blue sky and water. It's one of the most recognisable places on Earth from space because of the brightness of the water. Following a locally produced Croatian pilot book that contains charts of 777 harbours and anchorages, we discover beautiful sheltered bays. Stupica, Smokvica and Luka Zut all have restaurants selling their own caught fish at a very high price. Elizabeth and Heinz are great company during this leg; Heinz never left the wheel, enjoying this magic cruising ground immensely.

Kornati Islands

Biograd to Dubrovnik

It's now early September and time to stretch our legs. We join a fleet of around 24 charter cruising yachts for seven races over two weeks, from Biograd to Dubrovnik, 120 miles down the coast. The rally is run by Trevor Joyce's Mariner Boating Holidays and 134 people are here from Australia for the experience of sailing in a fleet, meeting in the evenings for dinner, and on lay days exploring the beautiful islands on their own. It promises to be an adventure, and we look forward to catching up with fellow Australians.

The race days offer up a mixed bag of conditions. The first race, to the Kornati Islands, is in perfect conditions; we're third across the line and win on handicap. *Cádiz* has never raced before, and considering we have a lot of gear on board we are surprised at how well she went. If Ian had written this he would tell you it's all skill, but of course I'm telling you it's the all-girl crew. The wind is shifty for the next couple of races, but then it's 12 knots on the nose, the strongest to date. I want to take some photos, but we're in trouble at the start

line and there's no one else to blame. We recover well and finish third, ranking again first on handicap.

The next race is abandoned due to no wind, and then it's the ladies' skipper day – it's not going to be me. Rebecca Hayter, editor of *Boating New Zealand*, takes the helm in little wind and now we're coming third. Ian wakes up sore the next day from all the grinding involved in crew work. On the final race to Dubrovnik, the wind dies and the race is abandoned with us in the lead. We win on points, and Bill Whisker from Perth gets the lowest points for a charter yacht.

The lay days are wonderful times of exploration, eating well and making new friends. En route to Primosten, our spinnaker gets its first airing since being repaired – it holds together and we have a very pleasant sail. On Trogir we all have a memorable dinner of cured ham, mussel and squid-ink risottos, and other platters of meats and fish. It's prize-giving time again and our cellar is filling up with Croatian

Croatia regatta

wine. We walk the narrow stone lanes of Trogir and admire the view from the old Venetian fort, including all our fleet tied up to the town dock. In the afternoon we find the bay of Krknjas on the island of Veli Drvenik and spend the evening surrounded by clear green water.

The ACI marina on the island of Saint Klement is fabulously located among the pine trees and we have another great dinner overlooking the bay. Crossing again to Hvar with the Saalfeld family and Bob Fraser's crew on board, some climb to the castle and others just sit in the sun, watch the passing parade, eat more food and drink more wine. The afternoon is spent in the bay of Soline and we are stern to in the clearest water to date. We can see quite clearly the weed-like grass 12 metres below us. It's great to catch up with so many sailing colleagues from Sydney and down a few glasses at the great functions after each race day. We need the lay days to recover from both activities.

In Korčula (again), everyone ventures out into the streets

of this wonderful old town. We moor alongside Bob's crew in a bay near a monastery with the mountain range behind. As the sun sinks into a magnificent sunset, we have cocktails on the bow. Our crew hire a car in Pomera and explore the island, while we cycle around the lake and lunch in a lakeside fish café. An ancient lady offers us some golden peaches with a heavenly fragrance. When I ask for her photo, she straightens her black scarf and gives me a gummy smile.

We spend the penultimate day in the inlet of Ston, visiting the old Roman saltpans (still in use) and the high, narrow wall built by the Turks to protect what was, at the time, a very valuable commodity. This is the area for oysters and mussels and we have a great lunch under the guidance of Milan, the rally race director, who has now joined us. The final supper is in stunning Dubrovnik, overlooking the lit-up walled town from the Hotel Excelsior.

We have thoroughly enjoyed ourselves, making new friends and acquaintances. To quote John Messenger, most people

Trogir from the tower

IAN'S CRUISING NOTES

In Split, John Messenger left us with the latest copy of **Sydney Afloat** and we had a laugh about the anchoring tips. In the Med the safety swing would just not apply. For example, in a harbour we visited at Hvar, you free your anchor, put out all fenders and hope you all move at the same time. There were 30 yachts in a small bay at anchor, and the night we were there we had no wind and just had to wait for a bump. Also in the bay stern to, thank goodness, was **Independence** – one of the largest superyachts around and great for sheltering behind.

had been racing all winter and they came to cruise, while the only racing we have done in the past six months is beating charter yachts into the marina. We also became the medic yacht and spare parts centre, and our deck compressor dive gear was well used.

Thanks to our crew – Rebecca, Brian, Judy and Natalie – for their help. Ian loved catching up on all the New Zealand yachting gossip from Rebecca and we almost learnt how to speak Noo Zilund again. A special thanks to Bob and Sue Fraser, Bainy and Annie, Andrew Joseph and Sandy for being such great companions, and John Messenger and Margo for filling our yacht with leftover grog and food.

Dubrovnik to Zadar

Back up the coast we go again. Jane Waters (another old Christchurch friend of Ian's) and partner John join us for a week on the journey to Split. Our first night out is in Luka on the island of Sipan. We spy an Australian flag and moor stern to alongside, only to be joined by another boat flying a CYCA flag – a Beneteau 50 owned by Helen Lovett and Damien Moloney, who are doing something similar to ourselves. The English yachtie on the other side moans about the Aussie invasion, complaining that he's had to put up with it for the past week.

We're travelling this coast for the third time, and each time we get the wind on the nose. Just our luck. Finding new secluded coves to swim in and have lunch never seems to disappoint us, as they are all isolated and beautiful. We spot a bright orange starfish, quite a find in these generally barren waters. Jane and I discover herbs and delicious wild figs ashore while John prepares a gourmet lunch, but the uninvited wasps move us on very quickly.

In Hvar again, we devour our best lunch to date at Hannibal's – carpaccio fish, scampi and grilled squid. John received a text message from Sydney telling us to visit a restaurant in Split called Boban … just as we sail into Split. Isn't technology great? While exploring the town, we ask a taxi driver what Split is famous for. He replies, 'Spit-roast lamb, black wine and someone else's wife. You can change to white wine if you like, but can't change the wife.'

Split's old town is within the walls of the fortified Diocletian Palace, a great example of late Roman (around AD 300) architecture. The city is the main commercial port in Croatia and also the main sailing centre. While we are in town, the national Optimist-class racing is on and it's great to see so many young girls and boys competing, even in these windy conditions. It's also good to catch up with Borut, the Musto agent here who we have known for years.

The temperature plummets as the bora (a strong local north-easterly) hits, fortunately while we are tied up in the marina. Jane and John catch the ferry to Italy and we intend

Croatia regatta: Trogir

to stay only one night in Split, but this turns into two as the bora lingers. We don't mind the wind, but the sudden cold snap is taking us by surprise.

Sunday is departure day and Ian is in his element in this wind, sailing 35 miles in four hours. I am snuggled up back in my bear suit to keep warm – it's the end of September and summer is finally over. We find a beautiful sheltered bay on the island of Tijat for the night, but it's far too cold for swimming. Next day Ian spearheads another great sail to Biograd. Why is it that everyone around us has only one sail up with a big reef, and we are charging along with both sails set and a small reef? We're first into the marina; I think Ian is still in the abandoned races from the Croatia rally.

During our last week, we visit the islands of Pag and Rab, north of Zadar. Though the weather has picked up, the tourists have gone and the place is deserted. Returning to Zadar, we discover a very impressive town, full of history and the best shops we have seen in Croatia. The Romans built the town on a peninsula and thankfully, many invasions later, Zadar still has a lot of its original architecture. The religious museum beside the cathedral run by the nuns is a must-visit. How such a priceless collection can survive the wars, especially the heavy Allied bombing at the end of World War II, is a tribute to the nuns who hid the artwork every time the area was invaded.

We wake on our last morning on board to a very thick fog, something we have not experienced since the Strait of

Gibraltar last year. *Cádiz* is now out of the water, high and dry in Marina Dalmacija at Sukosan, five miles south of Zadar. The largest marina in Croatia, it has 1200 marina berths and a further 1200 dry berths on land. It is very professionally run and we are happy wintering *Cádiz* here.

Six months, 3900 nautical miles travelled, 544 engine hours and six countries visited. Our eastern Med 2004 season is over. We still love each other and occasionally don't talk, but all in all it's a great experience to share. It seems daunting when we look back at what we have done and where we are going, but I've learned to take one day at a time and wouldn't miss it for anything. Next year we will travel north to Venice before sailing back to the western Mediterranean to cruise along the coastlines of the Italian and French Riviera.

Postscript

High in the Austrian Alps, our surroundings are a stark contrast to those of the past six months. We have now slept in a bed, showered with continuous water and pressed a button to flush the toilet. We're spending a few days with old friends Penny and Gerhard Fischer, who recently purchased a guesthouse/restaurant/bar in Dienten, in the Hochkoenig Valley near Salzburg, where there is a T-bar in the back yard just waiting for the snow season to begin.

ZADAR TO ROME

Zadar to Novigrad

We learn our lesson from last year's chilly start and wait until late May to begin our next Mediterranean sojourn. We clean up *Cádiz* and head back to Biograd to pick up friends Penny and Gerhard Fischer, who are joining us on the boat for two weeks, and also to catch up with friend Milan Sangulin, a partner in Marina Kornati who kept an eye on *Cádiz* over winter.

The last day of the Austrian Cup is on so, Ian being Ian, we follow the competitors out to the Kornati Islands. Austria is landlocked, but they still have a yacht club with 8000 members. This is one of four regattas they hold each year.

The weather is beautiful but calm, so already our average for motoring is high. Sailing north on the Adriatic Sea, we head for the remote and beautiful islands of Silba and Olib. The beach is made from hard white slate, so Gerhard builds a fire and the stone is our hotplate for cooking bratwurst. Eaten from slate 'plates', the barbecue is delicious and disposable. One of the nicest inlets is found on the island of Losinj in the bay of Krivica. It's surrounded by tall pine trees and once-loved stone houses that have been left to ruin.

We motor 40 miles through oily seas to the Istria Peninsula and the port of Pula. On one side of the marina is the majestic Roman amphitheatre, and on the other a boring new apartment block. The amphitheatre was built by Claudius for staging gladiator fights and held 23,000 people.

It's Saturday, and our new-found form of entertainment in the square is watching weddings. Every 15 minutes a new party arrives by car, amidst a mêlée of rice throwing, horns blowing and piano accordions playing. It's all very ethnic, even among the aroma of the sewage.

Out from Pula are the Brijuni Islands, a national park where President Tito, the former Yugoslav leader, had his summer residence and where even today the secrets of the communist era are strictly guarded. It's our plan to stay and enjoy the parklands and archaeological sites, but not at €90 for one night in the port. Our negotiations fail even to grant us a few hours on land, so we see the islands from the sea.

The stunning town of Rovinj restores our spirits. Its top-heavy cathedral and terraced, pastel-coloured houses squeeze onto a narrow peninsula. Steep meandering lanes and cobbled squares lead up to the cathedral, which houses the remains of Saint Euphemia. In AD 304 the teenage girl was fed to the lions by a Roman emperor for being a Christian. We would love to stay longer in the so-called 'blue pearl of the Adriatic'.

Gerhard has his first taste on the helm as we sail to Novigrad, which is to be our departure point for Venice. The days are breathlessly hot, 40°C and it's only late May. Tony Schmaehling, a former Sydneysider who's competed in seven Sydney–Hobart yacht races, started the Gamekeeper restaurant in Crown Street, and is now living in a fabulous renovated farmhouse in the hills behind Novigrad. We are honoured to spend a night ashore at his house in this wonderful fertile part of the Istrian coast.

The seafood here is excellent, and with the influence of Italy so close by, we find eating out a much more enjoyable experience. The mussels, tomatoes, ricotta and prosciutto are all worthy of a mention, although the area is famed for its black and white truffles (of the fungal variety).

Tony takes us sightseeing to the ancient Istrian town of Motovun, situated on a hilltop surrounded with boundary walls of grey stone and unforgettable views down the lush green valley. We lunch at the famous truffle restaurant Zigante, dining on truffle risotto, truffle pasta and truffle carpaccio with a local Malvazija white wine. Fearing overkill, we decline the white-chocolate mousse with black truffle. Back to the boat for our last night on the Croatian coast, we become the backdrop for a German TV crew as they film scenes for a documentary about local musicians and songs.

Marina Dalmacjia, Croatia

IAN'S CRUISING NOTES

When bringing our boat out of hibernation, we always paint the bottom with anti-fouling before putting her back in the water. As we are only in the water for four months, I only apply one coat with another around all the leading edges to stop paint building up. We use International Micron Extra, which doesn't deteriorate whilst out of the water. Andrea and I also polish the decks and sides, run up all the halyards and put the sails, bimini and dodger (sun and storm protectors) back in place.

Roman amphitheatre at Pula, Croatia

San Giorgio from San Marco, Venice

Venice to Sicily

There's no sign of wind so we leave early the next morning. And what an amazing scene meets our eyes as we enter Venice! The narrow canal is chaotically busy, with ocean liners, ferries, superyachts, small crafts and lots of markers leading the way but no such thing as port and starboard. Ian says 'Take the wheel' and I do, thinking he has to check the navigational charts. But then we hear from the galley, 'Cup of tea anyone?' It's strange how when something tricky or potentially embarrassing is going to happen, often it's either 'I need to go to the toilet' or 'Cup of tea?'.

We don't tie up to the poles in the canal; it's too choppy and will be uncomfortable. There's a private sailing club on the island of San Giorgio Maggiore, in sight of the famous Piazza San Marco, and if someone is away and you talk sweetly they will let you use someone's berth (for a fee, naturally). We're lucky to get in and stay four nights rafted to another yacht, as we are too wide to fit between their poles.

With an Antipodean mixture of cheek and naivety on our side, we cross the Grand Canal in our rubber dinghy to see

what happens. To our surprise it's no problem, so we join the queues of gondolas moving up the canals, under the Rialto Bridge and the Bridge of Sighs. On one gondola, a musician serenades the passengers with a piano accordion rendition of Sinatra's 'My Way'. A wedding passes by; we take photos of them and they take photos of us. It's all very friendly and people couldn't be nicer, directing us when we become lost in the maze of canals. Passing an Internet café, we tie up to read our emails. We learn later you may enter the canals in your own dinghy, but only in the afternoon when the markets have closed. Venice is still romantic, even when swarming with tourists in the evening. During our second night, the Piazza San Marco floods – an almost daily occurrence due to the square sinking and the sea invading at high tide.

Penny has her car here so we take a day trip inland to see Lake Garda and Verona. Romeo and Juliet's balcony gets only a brief look, as the first Italian fashion offerings of the season are more interesting. We aren't used to the fast highways and are very pleased to get back to the boat.

Rialto, Venice

Penny and Gerhard leave us in Venice; we have a busy morning finding laundry facilities to change the sheets, and then more guests arrive. Pip and Geoff Lavis (owners of the Sydney-based 50-foot yacht UBS *Wild Thing*) and Kevin Horne, also from Sydney, join us for three weeks of adventuring. For their benefit, we repeat our experience up the canals in the inflatable, and the waves are practically lapping over the side, but once in the canals, all is calm.

Due to a cold spell we are all rugged up; looking like we're about to enter the Sydney–Hobart Yacht Race, we hit the Adriatic nautical highway south at speed. It's 220 miles to our first stop, an outlying Croatian island called Vis, where we squeeze in at the village wall amongst many charter yachts and complete the hours of inevitable paperwork.

During the night the Bora wind blows 50 knots, but this doesn't keep Geoff, Kevin and Ian in port. We are the only yacht to pull out (gulp). Brindisi is only 160 miles away, Pip loves this stuff and I keep taking my seasickness pills. A wave hits the stern and flicks the inflatable dinghy out, even

though it's tied side on and up on the transom. 'All hands on deck!' goes up the cry. We're all there in a flash to retrieve the dinghy and outboard – luckily only the fuel tank and oars are gone. No one gets much sleep overnight and the autopilot is working overtime, but *Cádiz* sails very well in the lumpy sea. Thankfully we're going with the wind and not against it.

Geoff, Pip and Kevin have a quick lesson on the radar to ensure we're not on a collision course when re-entering the shipping lanes. After a rough night we make the calm waters of Brindisi's harbour at 6 am, in time to catch the start of the 100-mile Brindisi to Corfu yacht race. The day is spent provisioning and enjoying lunch – Puglia *orecchiette* pasta with seafood, washed down with a cold beer and some local wine.

There's no time to enjoy the countryside – we're off again before nightfall to catch the last of this front from the north to get us around the heel and under the sole of Italy's boot, into the Ionian Sea. The wind is turning to the south in a few days and that doesn't suit us, although hopefully it will bring hot weather from the African coast.

Sicily to the Aeolian Islands

Sicily, here we come! It's a very pleasant 250-mile motor-sail to Taormina, taking two nights and one day. This is the time to relax, read, eat and drink a wine or two. We're loving the olive bread, gorgeous Gorgonzola, cherry tomatoes like bunches of grapes, and wines at only €3 a bottle. So much for Geoff saying he doesn't drink at sea.

As we come within sight of the Sicilian coast at daybreak, a perfect view of snowcapped, smoking Mount Etna greets us. Apparently the grand old lady isn't visible very often, and she soon disappears behind the cloud. The small bays beneath Taormina aren't suitable for anchorage, as the tourists boats have taken over. Heading south for a few miles, we find a larger, calm bay at Porto Naxos (Giardini).

Taormina is described as the most beautiful town in Italy, with antiquities and a Greco-Roman theatre. Navigating the local transport is frustrating, but we find our way up the rocky bluff and are rewarded. The car-free main street, Corso Umberto, reveals antique shops, designer wear and coffee shops filled with marzipan fruits and pastries. Our eyes feast on beautiful contrasts of old grey stone against modern stainless steel, while overhead are wrought-iron balconies, iron clocks and carvings.

Time to do what Italians do best: passing the time with a coffee (delicious cappuccinos for us) and an almond biscuit. It's now very hot and we forgo seeing the theatre in favour of a pizza and cold beer, and then a siesta. Rather than battle with public transport again, we take taxis in the evening. Eating at Ristorante Da Nino, although costly, is delicious – a meal of small red prawns, steamed mussels, swordfish, tomato and eggplant pasta, and pistachio *gelato* to finish.

We head north through the narrow Strait of Messina, where Italy kicks Sicily into the sea. It's blowing 20 knots from dead astern, and we don't miss a beat holding on to our drinks. Watch out for the ferries, and for the whirlpools.

Decisions, decisions! Where to go – east or west? Sardinia or up the west coast of Italy? The west coast wins, via the Aeolian Islands, Tropea, the Amalfi coast and Capri.

We arrive at the island of Vulcano and anchor among other yachts on the west side, in time for the sunset. After a very physical climb to the smoking crater the next day, we return to sea level for a sulphuric mud bath and a blissful swim in the bubbling hot sea. Kevin discovers the wisdom of wearing shoes when jets of steam suddenly burst from the ground.

The main port in these islands is Lipari, and here we wash volcanic ash off the boat. After another siesta, we go by dinghy into the village for dinner. The village comes alive with teenagers parading in their latest clothes, boys with black spiked glossy hair, young children playing ball in the square with Coke cans, and locals going about their everyday rituals.

Stromboli is puffing smoke with lava running down the side. It's a wonderful contrast: one side is jet black, the other is green with yellow wildflowers. Rounding Stromboli as if she were a mark on a sailing course, we turn back towards the coast of Italy. Tropea's cliff-top houses, 200 steps up from the very pleasant marina, look like they've grown out of the rock, and Pip and I have a wonderful morning swim beneath them. This is onion country and Ian is teasing me because all we came for is the onion jam.

Another Australian yacht, *Caperata*, pulls in beside us with Mike Edgar and Jacqueline Woodhead and their big Alsatian dog Texas on board. It's a lovely surprise – they tell us we are the very reason they are here. We don't know these people, but they'd been reading our travel letters posted on www.sail-world.com. All Texas wants is to get ashore after holding his bladder for the entire overnight sail.

We leave Tropea with onions (of course), onion chilli jam, pickled onions and plaited fresh onions hanging in the yacht. And no, onion breath hasn't destroyed any friendships.

Mount Etna, Sicily

IAN'S CRUISING NOTES

When preparing our first-aid kit, we went well armed with the help of our doctor and pharmacist, although we found that all prescription drugs are freely available in most Mediterranean countries (as long as you can show them the box you want). We also carry Stugeron, a European seasickness pill not available in Australia or New Zealand, which works for most people without side effects. When sailing overnight we take it as a preventative measure, because if one of us goes down it wouldn't be easy to manage.

The yacht is fitted with a Brookes and Gatehouse automatic pilot, the best unit I've ever used. The computer drives an arm attached to a quadrant at the top of the rudder. The autopilot can be set to a compass course to your destination, a waypoint (a precise location on a chart) or a wind angle course. I prefer to use the waypoint, as the course doesn't correct itself as much as a compass course and uses less power. We use the autopilot 95 per cent of our time at sea and it steers as well as anyone.

Pizza at Taormina

Taormina

Amalfi coast to Ponza

Leaving at midday in a thunderstorm (anything for a bit of excitement), we set the sails and head for the Amalfi coast, 130 miles away. We've also acquired more red wine at a mere €1.80 per bottle, so by lunchtime we are a very happy bunch. Thanks to the vintage of all on board, we have the best music and we rock 'n' roll our sailing miles away.

After a beautiful roast lamb dinner while at sea, we stop at the small village of Palinuro for a short sleep and swim. It turns out to be the best swim of the season. Palinuro was recommended by an Italian couple who are also cruising, and I must say our best source of information is still just chatting to our fellow yachties.

Ian suggests we shower on our way into the port of Amalfi and Pip disappears below deck. Some time later, she peers out the porthole and all we hear are exclamations of amazement. Nestling in the valley between enormous mountains rising straight out of the sea, Amalfi is at her colourful best as the sun goes down. Ravello township perches high on a cliff above grapevines and lemon trees crossing the rugged mountain sides. Pastel-coloured houses and the gold- and green-tiled dome of San Andrea Church lie behind a small port full of fishing boats, yachts tied up to the wall, ferries coming and going. And then they squeeze in the superyachts. It's busy. The church has remains of the prophet St Andrew in a casket: interesting, considering that across the Mediterranean we have seen a number of churches making the same claim.

We are lucky to get a place on the wall and are soon cocooned between the fishing boat *St Andrea* and a 82-foot Dufour called *Wild Salmon*. Next to come in is the big one: a 130-foot 'mini ship' with 10 staff and – wouldn't you know it – off get just one couple. We're happy, as it makes a great surge breaker and we will get a good night's sleep. The war over power points is on again; Geoff spies someone pulling out our plug to use his and Ian moves ever so fast. Get in early, and don't let the bigger boats with the paid crew take control. We spend the evening sitting in the square devouring the very best *gelato*.

It's the middle of June and the weather is perfect, so we're slowing down to enjoy this part of Italy. The sea is flat and occasionally, if we're lucky, we get to sail in a light breeze of 12 knots. This area has its own version of the monsoon – every night for a very short time, black clouds form and it pours with rain.

Next day we cruise slowly up the Amalfi coast to Positano. Rugged mountains tower overhead with a road clinging to the cliff face. Buses take up the whole road on the corners, and you can hear their horns in and out of the tunnels. Hotels, mansions and restaurants dot the coast. With the bougainvillea in full bloom, it's an amazing sight.

Glorious Positano, and I'm glad we're on a boat. We leisurely lunch on board and drink in the scenery, before tackling the tourists and heat to explore this carless village. Climbing the only stairway in, we pass the usual tourist shops full of blue and yellow china and lemon-scented candles, all set under a cooling archway of pink bougainvillea. Ian passes the restaurant that ripped him off last year and mutters, 'I will get you one day.' Back at the boat, we all fall into the sea to cool off; what a relief.

On our way to Capri for the night, we see a lot of yachts anchored off an island and detour to have a look. The whole island belonged to the late Rudolf Nureyev – with its burnt-orange mansion and chapel, it's not a bad summer spot. It's Saturday night in Capri and we haven't booked, so we're turned away. This is a first for us, so it's back to the mainland to find a bay for the night on the Sorrento Peninsula, under huge cliffs. We anchor and Kevin takes a line ashore, lassoing a rock with a lot of difficulty, but it makes for a few laughs back at the boat while we watch.

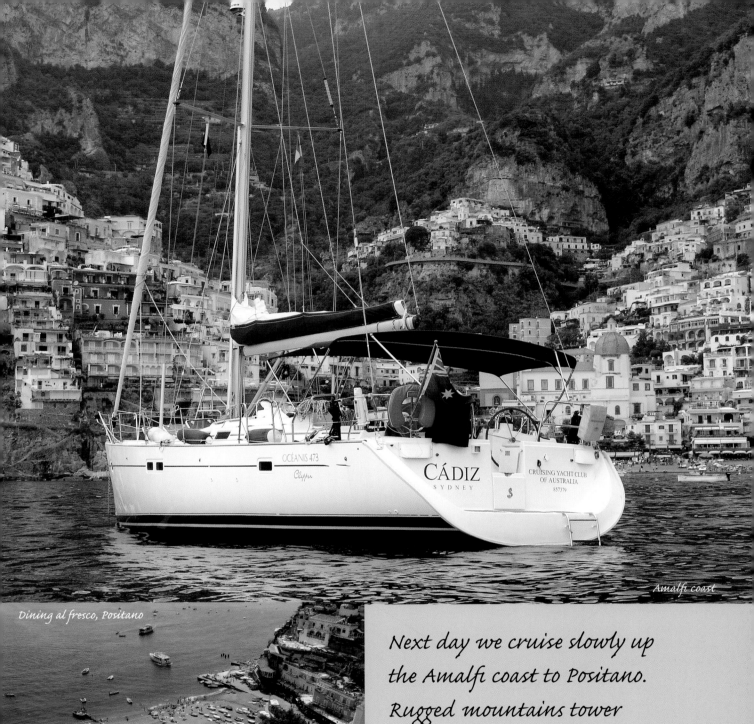

Amalfi coast

Dining al fresco, Positano

Next day we cruise slowly up the Amalfi coast to Positano. Rugged mountains tower overhead with a road clinging to the cliff face. Hotels, mansions and restaurants dot the coast.

Late afternoon traffic, Ponza

The sound of falling rocks is eerie, but with no one in sight and birds circling the cliffs, this is nature at its best.

Crossing back to Capri we anchor in Piccola, on the western side, in view of the Faraglioni Rocks. Surrounded by glistening cruisers and superyachts by the dozen, we spend the day swimming in sparkling water, then take up our reserved spot in the Capri marina, along with boats of every size. This is better than any boat show! Fast ferries arrive and depart by the minute – it's quite a circus – and we put all the fenders out so they can squeeze us in without damage. Taking the cable car up to the town, we join the rich and famous for the evening in Capri. It's fun to join in the people-watching, parading, admiring the shops and having drinks in the square.

As we leave Capri we motor up the coast to the famed Blue Grotto, and stop to see if they will take us off our boat and into the grotto. A big fat Italian, once a chef in Sydney, greets us with a hearty 'G'day' and rows us in his small boat to the even smaller entrance. Sitting on the floor behind him, I feel sure that if he fits, so will we. The grotto is indeed a beautiful blue, and he serenades us with 'Volare' ('Nel blu, dipinto di blu'). It's a shame the other five small boats in the grotto don't join in.

At nearby Ischia, another thermal resort island and one of the locations for the movie *The Talented Mr Ripley*, we stay the night and swim beneath Roman castles in emerald water. The islands off the Gulf of Naples are a beautiful cruising ground and we could spend more time here.

Ischia

Marina Grande, Capri

Ponza's small fishing village is full of colour, with pastel square houses and a harbour full of colourful fishing boats and yachts. Ian once again anchors in the front row, much to the amazement of Geoff and Kevin.

Football in the harbour, Ischia

Still, there's a breeze to catch, and all roads lead to Rome. Pausing for lunch at the island of Ventetene, we try to raise the anchor but the gears won't go into neutral. With three 'experts' on board a broken gear cable is diagnosed, and with Kevin in the engine room we get under way.

Sailing to the island of Ponza in flat calm seas – I swear it wasn't the lunchtime wine talking – we see a whale. A whale in the Tyrrhenian Sea? We all watch breathlessly as it spouts and the big tail rises. This is something we will never forget. I have since read that north of here is a vast area of sea, the Pelagos Sanctuary, established to protect whales and dolphins. It's great to see the three countries (Italy, France and Monaco) working together to help these mammals survive in an area of such intense commercial, military and cruising traffic.

Ponza's small fishing village is full of colour, with pastel square houses and a harbour full of colourful fishing boats and yachts. Ian once again anchors in the front row, much to the amazement of Geoff and Kevin. The restaurant EEA is a great find, and as restaurants are usually booked out four days in advance on Ponza, we're lucky to get a table. The waitress brings tuna carpaccio, octopus salad, Gorgonzola zucchini roulade, red prawns, marinated anchovies, eggplant mozzarella tomato stack, followed by fresh fish and tuna with a rosemary and olive tapenade. If it sounds fantastic, well, it is. In fact it's the best meal we've had ashore this year.

Back at the yacht we open the last bottle of limoncello to toast our last night with our guests on board. With sore heads the next morning, we set off for Rome.

Rome to the Tuscan islands

From one side of Italy (Venice) to the other (Rome), we sailed 1040 miles in three weeks together – and now Geoff and Pip Lavis, and Kevin Horne, leave us. Their company was wonderful during our circumnavigation of the boot of Italy; we had a lot of laughs, ate good food and probably drank too much wine for our own good.

Porto Turistico di Roma is becoming a familiar haunt for us, and it's turning into an upmarket resort with 800 boat spaces filled with a lot of very powerful boats. Ian gets the gear cable fixed and I'm happy taking in the fashion boutiques. Italy is in the grip of a heatwave, and temperatures are well into the 40s. A day trip into Rome isn't a good idea in this heat, but we have our favourite shops and the wine bar L'Enotec Antica, in Via della Crose, to visit. People queue to get into the Gucci shop; there are policewomen wearing stilettos. There's always something different to see in Rome.

You hear a lot about Tuscany, but never much about the Tuscan islands. There are seven islands in total between Corsica and Italy, covering a distance of 70 miles north to south. The low-lying small Isola di Giannutri, a national park, is 60 miles north of Rome, making it a favoured weekend spot for all the boats from Rome. Anchoring in deep crystal-blue water, we find the bay is full of both boats and thousands of birds. What noise! There's no stereo at sunset tonight; the mother gulls are trying to get their babies to sleep and that's enough racket for us all. Hitchcock's movie *The Birds* looms large in my mind, and I don't dare feed them.

The island of Giglio is 12 miles north, a much higher island of solid granite. A bay close to the port is paradise – it doesn't get any cleaner and clearer than this. The port is small but quaint, daubed in Tuscan colours and golden sand. We visit the mountain-top castello (old town) by bus and make the mistake of going at midday. First, it is incredibly hot; second, the bus drivers also have a siesta (we never get used to the siesta thing) and we get temporarily stranded up the mountain. But it's a charming place to visit. The medieval stone-walled castle is still intact, and people still live inside the defensively clustered houses. Narrow alleyways, arches and hanging pot plants in flower lead to the Parish Church.

Breakfast ashore consists of cappuccino and melt-in-the-mouth chocolate croissants. Two please! We motor-sail past the island of Montecristo (out of bounds to yachts) and on to Elba, the biggest of the islands, for more bay-hopping, eating and swimming. Napoleon was exiled to Elba for two years, so we visit his mansion with beautiful gardens and great views; not a bad place to be exiled to, all in all. These islands are an Italian secret, and they say there is great diving to be had. We also hear that inland Elba is interesting, and make a note to return someday to see more of this mountainous island.

Our first mistral wind warning comes in the bay of Portoferrio – one of the safest ports in the Mediterranean, according to Lord Nelson. It's not too bad a wind but we drag anchor while we are away from the boat, creating a surprise on our return. Roddy on a neighbouring yacht boards *Cádiz* and lets out more anchor. It turns out we have our anchor on a sunken tarpaulin. Just as well we're not in the Gulf of Lion, where it's blowing 50 knots. Portoferrio is home to one of the America's Cup syndicates, Mascalzone Latino, and next year the Farr 40 World Championships are in the next bay along, Porto Azzurro. We meet up with Franco and Livia Pivoli, the Musto agents for Italy, who assure us that dinner ashore is going to be good. And it is – Moreton Bay bug spaghetti and fish soup. Yum.

On our way to La Spezia, Ian takes a nap in our cabin in the bow, little knowing that dolphins are playing just a few feet underneath him. It doesn't matter how often I encounter dolphins, they never fail to enchant me, and it's always nice to stop what I'm doing and enjoy them.

RECIPES **ITALY**

ROAST LAMB WITH CHERRY TOMATOES

1 leg or rack of lamb, about 700 g
2 cloves garlic, peeled and cut
*   into 6 slivers*
sea salt
olive oil
6 small waxy potatoes,
*   peeled and diced*
2 Spanish red onions,
*   peeled and quartered*
4 cloves garlic, unpeeled
2 lemons, halved
3 fresh sprigs rosemary,
*   or 2 tsp dried herbs*
½ cup water
1 bunch cherry tomatoes on vine

Preheat oven to 160–180°C. With a small, sharp knife make 6 cuts in lamb and push a sliver of garlic into each. Place lamb in an oven pan, sprinkle with salt and oil and cook for 1 hour. Remove from oven and surround lamb with potato, onion, garlic and lemon (flesh down). Sprinkle with rosemary and more olive oil. Pouring a little water into the base of the pan will prevent burning. Return lamb and vegetables to oven for 30 minutes. Near the end of cooking time place the tomatoes (still on vine) on top of the lamb to warm through. Transfer lamb to platter and rest for 10 minutes. Slice and surround with potatoes and onions. To the excess liquid in the pan, add squeezed lemon and garlic pulp. Stir, then strain over lamb.

SWEET CHERRY TOMATO SALAD

10 cherry tomatoes, halved
2 Tbsp apple cider vinegar
1 clove garlic, peeled and
*   crushed*
3 Tbsp extra virgin olive oil
fresh basil, roughly chopped
sea salt to taste

Combine first 5 ingredients in a small bowl and add pinch of sea salt.

GORGONZOLA FETTUCCINE PASTA

150–200 g fettuccine pasta
sea salt
2 cloves garlic, peeled and
*   crushed*
2 Tbsp olive oil
30 g Gorgonzola cheese, diced

Cook fettuccine in salted boiling water. When 'al dente', drain and set aside. Heat oil and garlic in pasta pot. Return pasta to the pot. Stir through Gorgonzola and serve.

Tuscan islands

Coffee break

Giglio

GEORGE'S MOJITO

All credit to George Snow for this cocktail, which is very refreshing on a hot day … and kicks like a burro.

1 bunch mint
60 ml brown rum
½ lime, quartered
20 ml sugar syrup
ice
soda or tonic water

Place 8–10 mint leaves in a glass with rum and lime wedges. Pound with the end of a rolling-pin or similar utensil to release mint essence and lime juice. Add sugar syrup and ice, then top up with soda or tonic water.

MOZZARELLA AND TOMATO SALAD

This is easy in Italy, where there's always fresh mozzarella available. The best is made from buffalo milk, rich and creamy!

3 balls mozzarella, sliced
3 ripe tomatoes, sliced
handful fresh basil, roughly chopped
extra virgin olive oil
freshly cracked black pepper

On a serving dish, arrange alternating slices of mozzarella and tomato. Sprinkle with basil and drizzle generously with oil. Scatter over pepper to taste.

PRAWN PASTA

I find seafood irresistible and this dish is no exception. Use the heads and shells from the prawns to add extra flavour to the stock.

500 g green (uncooked) prawns, peeled

FISH STOCK
prawn shells
2 cups water
2 Tbsp tomato purée
4 cloves garlic, peeled and chopped
1 onion, peeled and chopped
herbs to flavour, e.g. oregano or rosemary
2 bay leaves
1 whole small red chilli
sea salt
freshly cracked black pepper

Combine all stock ingredients in a large pot. Bring to a boil, and simmer for 1 hour. Remove from heat and strain.

PASTA
200 g fettuccine pasta
sea salt
olive oil
4 cloves garlic, peeled and chopped
1 cup single cream
freshly cracked black pepper
½ bunch fresh coriander, chopped

Cook pasta in salted boiling water. When 'al dente', drain and set aside. Heat oil and garlic in pasta pot; add fish stock and cook prawns in stock for about 3 minutes until firm. Return pasta to the pot, stir cream through and serve. Season with pepper and top with chopped coriander.

FLAMING STRAWBERRIES

There's an art to setting light to this most perfect summer holiday dessert. Make sure the pan is hot; set light to it as soon as you've added the alcohol and use a long taper. If the dish doesn't light, it's probably not hot enough.

1 Tbsp brown sugar
1 Tbsp butter
3 cups strawberries, washed, hulled and halved
2 Tbsp fruit-flavoured brandy

In a heavy-based pan, heat sugar gently until pale brown (caramelised), then add butter. When butter is melted add strawberries and brandy and heat until bubbles begin to form around the edges. Light brandy just before serving; flames will die out when alcohol is burnt off. Serve with whipped cream.

Portovenere

La Spezia to Portofino

In La Spezia we meet up with our son Ian, who has flown in from Sydney, and our daughter Janey, who joins us from her job with Super-Maxi racing yacht *Maximus NZL99999* (currently in Cowes preparing for racing). It's nice to be back together as a family once again.

We love northern Italy and are moving very slowly, enjoying it all. The weather has had something to do with it too, as unseasonable lows are causing the mistral to enter the Gulf of Genoa. The Gulf of La Spezia on a hot summer Saturday is abuzz, full of yachts and hundreds of inflatables. Everyone is out on every imaginable type of boat to enjoy the beautiful harbour. La Spezia is a large commercial and naval port, but behind all this is a wonderful bustling pleasant town with great architecture. It is also the arrival point for the famed Cinque Terre villages, spread along the coast just north of the harbour.

Portovenere, at the entrance to the gulf, is a medieval village of houses jammed together between a stone church and a castle. It's renowned for basil pesto and mouth-watering pizzas. A reminder that the weather can still do anything: we plan to sail up the coast but have to wait out high winds in a small bay called Le Grazie. Ashore for our morning coffee, we find a delightful village and supermarket at which to provision.

A second night in Portovenere, which is no hardship, sees us enjoying what turns out to be a famous restaurant, Locanda Lorena, regularly graced by the stars. Set on the island of Palmaria, diners are picked up in a highly varnished boat from the mainland. Grilled whole scampi, mussels from the bay, marinated salmon – we're in seafood heaven. The seas are choppy and there's no wind – it's uncomfortable but we press on past small medieval villages clinging to cliffs. The Cinque Terre area consists of five picturesque coastal villages, all within a few miles of each other, which are linked by a famous walking track. The villages were built in valleys where the only access was by

Looking north to the Cinque Terre, Portovenere

Portovenere

sea, but train stations now sit on the edge of each village and you can walk through the streets from there. Once-abandoned terraces are being restored and vines adorn the cliff faces once again.

Anchoring off Vernazza (we are too long to fit into the small harbour), the most picturesque of the villages, we venture in by dinghy – a tricky feat in the swell. We just have time for a stroll along the terraces and wonder how steep cliffs could be terraced and cultivated for hundreds of years and yet remain fertile.

Our venue for lunch, and a welcome swim in surprisingly pale blue water, is the sheltered harbour of Sestri Levante, where Marconi first experimented with radio waves. Only 10 miles on, we're now alongside Rapallo, Santa Margherita and Portofino (all within 3 miles of each other), a popular holiday-home area for wealthy northern Italians. The wind is strong, with 50-knot winds still in the Gulf of Lion, and we're on the tail end of it. I'm starting to dread that part of the coast, but hopefully our timing will be in our favour.

Portofino entrances us for two nights as we shelter from the wind: this picturesque little port, surrounded by manicured gardens, sculpted trees, terraced pastel-coloured houses, and a few elegant mansions, is utterly perfect. We anchor in the bay just outside the port in very deep water; it's surging too much for us in the port. At first we're on our own, but we're soon surrounded by superyachts and locals in their highly varnished picnic day-boats. The port looks full – and then somehow they squeeze in more yachts. By the number of superyachts present, Portofino sure has a lot of appeal for such a small location.

Portofino

Portofino entrances us for two nights as we shelter there from the wind: this picturesque little port, surrounded by manicured gardens, sculpted trees, terraced pastel-coloured houses, and a few elegant mansions, is utterly perfect.

Day boats, Portofino

Waterfront, Portofino

Gelato for Janey

The port looks full – and then somehow they squeeze in more yachts. By the number of superyachts present, Portofino sure has a lot of appeal for such a small location.

Among the superyachts, Portofino

Vernazza, Cinque Terre

Portofino to Villefranche-sur-Mer

The sun comes back on day three, so we spend the day in Portofino people-watching and swimming before heading to Marina Santa Margherita to pick up George and Sabrina Snow, owners of the yacht *Brindabella* from Sydney. Eating out has become a joy – the seafood is fabulous, and we dine at di Beppe on the marina. We may never leave.

The wind has dropped and it's hot again, so we motor north along the Italian Riviera to Genoa. The coast is very exposed but still heavily populated – long stairways wind to the sea from mansions atop high cliffs.

We've read about the statue of Christ beneath the water in the bay of San Fruttuoso, and let me tell you, he's not easy to find. He appears in 15 metres of water, standing 4 metres high with arms stretched skyward; very scary to behold. Janey says she'll never forget the look on his face, and Ian comments that he looks like he wants to get to the surface.

Stopping for coffee at Camogli, a charming fishing village piled high with nets, George discovers that the name of this little port comes from the word for 'communal house',

where fishermen's wives were locked up until their return (thankfully this only happened a long time ago).

We may be in old-town Genoa (home to explorer Christopher Columbus), but we are parked in what might as well be the sewer – we diplomatically ask to be moved. Sabrina and I visit the must-see Chiossone Museum, with the largest Oriental exhibition in the Western world. George and Ian visit the Aquarium of the Sea and see first-hand a live ocean sunfish, a giant fish shaped like a vast disc. They now understand why a yacht stops if it hits a sunfish.

Everyone is at the coast for summer, and the beaches throng with umbrellas, deck chairs, changing sheds ... and people. At Varazze, we have to anchor in a bay and roll all night. This is not in the brochure! At Finale Ligure we sadly farewell Janey and Ian, who are on their way to London.

The only island (and a private one to boot) on this part of the coast is Isolotto Gallinara, but you can anchor and swim off it. I do so, until I encounter my first stinging jellyfish. I'm never too sure what to put on stings, but

When passing from one country to another, Spain, Italy and France are all quite casual, but the one rule you must observe is that a vessel can only stay in the European Union for 18 months before you are liable for VAT (sales tax). After 18 months you must take the vessel out of the EU for six months before you can re-enter for a further 18 months. This is getting more difficult as other countries are joining the EU, so your best options at the moment are Tunisia, Turkey and Croatia.

Marina Fontvieille, Monaco

vinegar comes to mind and seems to do the trick.

We visit Imperia Porto Maurizio only to see the pasta museum – but it's been relocated to Rome. Instead, while Ian and George check out the yachts, Sabrina and I find a new and impressive olive museum, Museo dell'Olivo. We catch a bus back but are kicked off for not having a ticket (you have to get your ticket at the tobacconist before boarding, but there were none in sight).

San Remo is a nonevent, and we continue moving, eating and drinking. George leads the way, especially with his ultra-strong Mojitos. I even saw him chased down the road after picking mint from a restaurant's garden.

Crossing the border to France, we stop in Menton, an attractive old town, and we can't believe the change. It's not only the language: the food and shops feel different too. I'm sure the coffee will never be as good as in Italy. Phoning ahead to reserve a spot in Monaco, we're told *Cádiz* is too small for the main marina. Our eventual destination, the Marina Fontvieille, has its own bonuses.

We're moored beneath and in view of Prince Albert's palace, and there's a fabulous Carrefour supermarket ashore. It has the best-quality supplies and is tax-free (we fill three shopping trolleys); how could we resist Côtes du Rhône at €2 a bottle?

Following the tourist trail, we tour the palace and see Prince Albert cross the courtyard; visit the cathedral where Princess Grace and Prince Rainer are buried; and check out the museum. However, no visit to Monaco is complete without an evening in the casino square, just sitting outside a café, watching the passing of people and the gleaming, growling supercars: red and yellow Ferraris, silver Rolls Royces and ice-blue Maseratis.

On Sunday, boats head to bays both north and south to enjoy this beautiful day. In the bay off Cap Ferrat, we weave our way in and out of superyachts, including one with two helicopters. Prestigious estates line the bays, and we stay the night off Villefranche-sur-Mer. George dubs this 'get drunk early day'. We politely join in.

Menton

Menton

Beachside, Juan-les-Pins

IAN'S CRUISING NOTES

The marina is the focal point in Antibes, and it's a major port on the Côte d'Azur for repairs and maintenance. A steady stream of superyachts based here left in the morning, and returned later in the day, making this port a very busy one.

Shelter was excellent on the Italian and French Riviera, so we stayed no more than two nights a week in marinas. Prices on the French Riviera were around €55 per night.

Antibes to St Tropez

The area between Antibes and Cannes is beautiful and we haven't moved very far in a few days. Antibes is a very old town, with narrow cobblestoned streets and the best market we have seen on this trip. I've never seen so many stalls bursting with cheeses, spices, oils, perfumes, antipasto, fruits and vegetables, all exquisitely displayed and creating a festival of fragrances. We buy far too much for the boat, but still eat out at a very French restaurant, Le Vauban, behind elegant lace in Rue Thuret. The food is presented beautifully and tastes as good as it looks.

Early riser George rouses us to see the Picasso Museum. Picasso painted in the town's castle for a short time in 1946 and left all his sketches here in Antibes. As the day heats up, we can't wait to get back out to sea and swim.

It seems like literally everyone is, indeed, on the water. We're bay-hopping around the Cap d'Antibes and we've never seen so many boats. It's a 'who's who' of superyachts, cruisers and topless females draped over bows. Keeping Ian and George focused on steering is difficult. A swell in this area from the open sea will mean an uncomfortable night in a bay, so we're thankful to get a space in Port Gallice/Juan-les-Pins, an upmarket and secluded resort town. The International Jazz Festival is on in Juan-les-Pins, so we enjoy an open-air evening performance by Stefano Di Battista from Italy and the McCoy Tyner All Stars from America.

The islands of Sainte Marguerite and Saint Honorat are only five miles away, but even mid-week they're crowded with boats in this pristine blue water. On the island of Sainte Marguerite is Fort Royal Prison, infamous for housing the mysterious 'Man in the Iron Mask' for 11 years — the man's identity is still unknown today. You can enter the prison cell, which is now a museum for locally found Roman artefacts.

The monastery on tiny Saint Honorat has been going since the fourth century. In its heyday this haven from the world was very influential, producing some 20 saints and 600 bishops. Saint Patrick studied here for nine years before going on to convert the Irish. Visitors can join the monks in prayer, wake at 4 am, work in the vineyards by day and not say a word. It wouldn't suit us!

Back up to Antibes, and Sabrina and George leave us, so we do the laundry, wash the boat, replenish the galley, and siesta in the afternoon. Evening drinks are with Martin and Bridget Grover, who have just launched their new Beneteau 473 and are off to see the Mediterranean. As you do …

Liz and Heinz are flying down from the Cognac region in France in their private plane for a third visit with us, bringing with them our son Ian. We meet them in Cannes and it happens to be Brazilian night, so we venture ashore. It only takes one huge trailer, 15 musicians, three dancers, six singers and 112 decibels of sound, and the whole town watches the truck inch down the promenade; we follow the beat of drums and the sight of people dancing in the street for some time.

The journey from Villefranche to St Tropez is especially enjoyable and prompts us to change our plans for August. Instead of continuing west to Spain, we're only going as far as Marseille and then sailing back along the coast to Monaco. Crossing 100 miles to Corsica, we'll aim for Sardinia by early September in time for the Maxi Yacht Rolex Cup (or 'Maxi Worlds'), as Ian is sailing on *Maximus*. That's the great thing about being on your own boat — you can change your plans.

We're loving this busy area, which hasn't been as costly as we expected. What has impressed us most is the clean, clear water and beautiful bays in which to anchor at night. And if you want the busy nightlife, the marinas are close at hand.

Bring on the glitz: we're in St Tropez. It's time for the highest heels, shortest skirts and most perfectly tanned bodies. We're looking forward to a few fabulous days surrounded by glamour.

Market, St Tropez

Antibes is a very old town, with narrow cobblestoned streets and the best market we have seen on this trip. I've never seen so many stalls bursting with cheeses, spices, oils, perfumes, antipasto, fruits and vegetables, all exquisitely displayed and creating a festival of fragrances.

RECIPES **FRANCE**

MOULES IN CURRY AÏOLI

Leftover aïoli is great with cold cuts.

MUSSELS
1 Tbsp butter
½ Spanish red onion,
  peeled and chopped
½ cup white wine
herbs to flavour
500g black mussels

In a large saucepan, melt butter
and add onion. Lightly cook for 5–7
minutes, then add wine and herbs.
Bring to a boil and add mussels. Cover
and cook for 10 minutes or until all
mussels have opened. (Discard any
unopened shells.) Transfer mussels to
serving bowl and set aside.
Add 2 tablespoons of the aïoli to the
pan and heat through. Pour liquid over
opened mussels and serve with French
bread.

AÏOLI
1 egg yolk
2 cloves garlic, peeled and crushed
½ tsp curry powder
½ cup extra virgin olive oil
juice of ½ lemon

Lightly whisk egg, add garlic and
curry. Slowly drizzle in oil, whisking
continuously until egg and oil are well
blended. Add lemon juice.

ROASTED LEMON COQUELET

Coquelets are small chickens, and you'll find
them in most good French supermarkets.

2–3 whole coquelets
6 potatoes, peeled and cubed
2 onions, peeled and quartered
4 cloves garlic, unpeeled
2 lemons, halved
bunch fresh or dried rosemary
olive oil
salt

Preheat oven to 175°C. Place chicken in a
roasting pan and surround with vegetables
and garlic. Add lemons, cut-side down. Sprinkle
with rosemary, olive oil and salt. Pour some
water into the base of pan to prevent anything
burning. Cook for 1 hour. Cut chickens in half
and arrange on a platter with vegetables.
Drizzle with juices from pan and from
squeezed lemons.

LEMON PASTA WITH TOMATO AND CHILLI

200 g penne pasta
sea salt
2 cloves garlic, peeled
1 small red chilli, deseeded
  and sliced
olive oil
½ lemon, rind on, finely sliced
1 tomato, chopped
grated Parmigiano Reggiano

Cook pasta in salted boiling water
until 'al dente'. Drain and set aside.
Gently heat garlic, chilli and oil in
pasta pot. Return pasta to the pot.
Add lemon and tomato and stir
through. Serve topped with grated
Parmigiano Reggiano.

Marseille

St Tropez to Le Lavandou

St Tropez certainly lives up to the reputation of being bigger than big, brighter than bright and glitzier than glitzy. How this little fishing village (it still is) became such an enormous attraction, I don't know, but it's well worth an extended visit. The promenade is lined with superyachts, artists selling paintings, restaurants and boutiques. The whole spectacle is entertaining, from your first coffee in the morning until your last drink at night. The speciality of the area is a cream puff called *tarte Tropezienne*, served with raspberries that really do taste like raspberries. Delicious.

St Tropez harbour offers great anchorage, as the marina is often full. We anchor out all the time as it's no trouble taking the dinghy ashore and being in the front row even if it is only our inflatable. We're pleasantly surprised to learn that, had we stayed in the marina, it would have cost only €64 a night. Liz, Heinz and young Ian leave us here, but we'll see them again sooner than we expect.

From St Tropez, we round the Cap de St Tropez to the glamour beaches and bars, called Tahiti-Plage, Bora Bora, Moorea, and the like. The orange-and-white striped sun loungers, matching beach umbrellas, bars, restaurants and bikini shops are all on the beach; this is extreme sophistication. Ian is in his element, sitting at the bar, sunglasses on and head swinging. There's even a casual fashion parade going through the bar. I forgot my high heels, but sandy bare feet and a glass of rosé in hand feel pretty good.

Sailing south, it is a beautiful day so we anchor overnight off the nearby bay of Briande. The morning brings a wind and Ian gets up to check if we are holding still, only to see two other boats drift out to sea. The occupants on one wake up and return, but the other one? Who knows. Last night it rained a little and the boat became unbelievably dirty, apparently due to red dust from the Sahara that is blown up into the atmosphere and comes down when it rains.

A mistral wind is forecast for the next four days, so we head for shelter in one of the many marinas along the coast. Phoning ahead, we find many are booked out, but in Le Lavandou in Provence they just say 'First in, first served.' We move in, tie up and wait for our first mistral. It's hot, dry and dusty, and will blow to 40 knots. Le Lavandou, named after the local lavender fields, boasts a cute town with golden beaches and holiday-makers. Lunch is a huge bowl of black mussels in wine sauce with a touch of curry, soaked up with baguettes.

In the marina we catch up again with English couple Roddy and Sue Stevens on their 10-metre motor sailer. After 20 years of summering here, they're finally selling their berth and boat – they're in their seventies and are ready for something new. Ian changes the oil and everything else, loving the chandlery at the end of our pier. When the floorboards are up the men couldn't be happier, and during breaks from writing this I have to admire dirty filters and pump old oil.

The mistral keeps up, so we leave *Cádiz* and fly to Cognac to stay with Liz and Heinz. They have a beautiful home and a small vineyard where they grow their own grapes to produce 4000 bottles of sauvignon blanc for private use. The wine is very drinkable, with no additives, and was especially good with the black mussels Heinz cooked in their wine with some herbs.

Life wouldn't be normal if we didn't get on the water, so we hire canoes and paddle 10 kilometres down the Charente River, opting to shoot the many rapids instead of walking around the locks, causing many laughs and a few rescues. Swans, vineyards, old stone homes and castles, and people on their homely barges slide by. We pick wild blackberries among the weeping willows, something I haven't done since I was in New Zealand. A week ago we were simply sailing along the coast and had never heard of Le Lavandou; now we feel like locals. It's a long journey, via plane, bus, train and bus again, back to our boat.

The promenade is lined with superyachts, artists selling paintings, restaurants and boutiques. The whole spectacle is entertaining, from your first coffee in the morning until your last drink at night.

St Tropez

IAN'S CRUISING NOTES

Seagrass is a serious problem in the Mediterranean and makes anchoring very difficult. We sometimes spent ages looking for a sandy patch to drop our anchor. Having dragged a few times, we decided it was wise to purchase a bigger anchor. We had a 20 kilogram (45 lb) CQR, the recommended size for our yacht, but our new 30 kilogram (65 lb) CQR solved all our problems. We have 100 metres of 10-millimetre chain, and often let out 50 metres. Once we dug it in, we pulled up some chain so we didn't drift into other yachts at anchor in the bay. Weed grass (as we encountered in Briande) can be over a metre high – sometimes the bottom looked very rocky, but it turned out to be different levels of weed.

The mistral blows from the north out of the Rhône valley. It's mentioned often, but this is the first wind we have had in our time on the Riviera. The mistral really only blows hard once you're west of St Tropez and into the Rhône Delta past the port of Marseille.

Port Miou, Les Calanques

Les Calanques to Marseille

Local knowledge is to thank for our next port of call – many fellow sailors and locals told us about Les Calanques, between Marseille and Cassis. The calanques are steep miniature fiords carved out of white limestone over the ages. Our pick is Calanque d'En Vau: long and narrow with a wonderful pebble beach at the end, 50-metre high cliffs all around with pines growing out of rock cracks. It's 10 metres deep right up to the cliff edge, and the water is exceptionally clear and cold. Fresh spring water flows into the bay through the limestone seabed. This is paradise ... and so is the glamour on visiting yachts.

With anchor down and a line ashore to one of the many rings attached to the cliffs, we feel secure for the night alongside several other yachts. Then the mistral returns and yachts start to drag. We hadn't let out much chain in the narrow fiord, so we drag and have to anchor again. With gusts of 40 knots we are often on our side, and I'm holding onto the side of the bed. At one stage there's a calamity of noise; startled, we both bolt for the hatch, only to find that it was just another gust passing over. Ian loves this and dreams all night that he's in the Sydney–Hobart race, while I stay awake watching all the boats depart. By daybreak we are the only yacht left.

Travelling on to Marseille, we stop at several other picturesque calanques with the same icy water. Calanque de Sormiou is famous for the 1991 discovery of an underwater cave, now 36 metres below the surface, with prehistoric paintings dating back to 20,000 BC.

Marseille, despite what people say, is a clean harbour and an interesting city. The local yacht club arranges a berth right in the heart of the old port and town. The town is vibrant, with a mixture of people from all the past French colonies. Young Ian has now joined us again and will sail back up the coast with us.

We dine ashore to sample the authentic Marseille *bouillabaisse* (fish stew). It is very good, but restaurants

Beautiful Calanque d'En Vau

like to have your booking 24 hours in advance in order to create a truly excellent dish.

Marseille wouldn't be complete if we didn't visit the island just off the port. The magnificent Château d'If standing guard was the fictitious prison in Alexandre Dumas' *The Count of Monte Cristo* (23 movies have been made of this novel). Anchoring off this rugged white-stone island, we let our imaginations run wild after a good tour of the prison cells, where the movies are continuously shown. We leave with the novel to read, understanding the hardships he would have undergone.

This is as far west as we go, so it's time to retrace our steps and revisit our favourite haunts along the coast to Monaco before we cross to Corsica. Wind, wind, wind, but finally it's blowing in the right direction. We're sailing in fresh winds of 30 knots all day, every day. It's fabulous.

Calanque de Sormiou

Artistic St Tropez

Marseille to St Tropez

Two more days pass as we introduce young Ian to the calanques. It truly is a beautiful area, but the wind is still a menace. According to the pilot book the Calanque Port Miou offers the best shelter; it's also where we have our worst night. We're secured to permanent moorings from both stern and bow, and we roll all night. There's nothing romantic happening tonight, I can assure you.

By day young Ian has me climbing the cliffs, diving and snorkelling, but I draw the line at daredevil jumps from the cliffs. The wind looks good for a fast sail and Ian is eager to put up the sails, so off we go at 4 pm, not intending to go far. Young Ian gleefully surfs along behind the boat in the dinghy, taking photos. At 8 pm and 40 miles later, I call it a day and we take shelter on the eastern side of Presqu'île de Giens. This is pink flamingo territory and next morning we go on a wild goose chase (as it were) in search of these beautiful birds. Three hours later, we return to the boat without seeing any flamingoes. Ian is not amused.

The Hyères Islands are near here and even though it's very windy, we sail across to the national park on the island of Porquerolles, a beautiful green island with walking and cycling trails, and a wonderful variety of trees (even some Australian eucalyptus). After a swim in the beautiful Nôtre Dame bay Ian decides we should find shelter from the wind and we sail back under blue skies to the mainland.

Not wanting to miss the last island in this group, we set off early to see Port Cros before the wind gets up. Port-Man harbour at the eastern end, with a fort at the entrance, is tranquil and full of boats. After a long walk to the fort, a wasp sting and a swim with the jellyfish, it's all too much and I would rather be sailing.

The beach at the Baie de Pampelonne behind St Tropez, made famous by local resident Bridget Bardot, is 30 miles away and by the time we get there the wind has died. The latest and greatest bar is Nikki Beach (apparently we just missed seeing Paris Hilton). You have to see it to believe it: huge outdoor white mattresses, matching umbrellas, and loud music. A 'water fight' with champagne is in progress beside the pool. Needless to say, it's not a place where a lot of clothing is worn.

The mistral is back with a vengeance, so we have another turbulent night at anchor off St Tropez. The gusts hit 40 knots. *Cádiz* lunges to one side and stretches the anchor chain to its very limit … and then we wait for the next gust. But thanks to our big anchor, we don't move.

We spend the morning watching mini Wally yachts (50-foot playthings for the rich and famous) match-racing around the harbour, and then have a glitzy night out in St Tropez where a single round of drinks costs €70. Expensive, sure, but it's still a very beautiful place to be.

Nikki Beach bar

Tahiti Plage

Superyachts, St Tropez

St Tropez to Monaco

We find it too hard to leave St Tropez, so we stay a little longer. Ahh, freedom. The weather is perfect: it's a surprisingly mild August, and even the nights are cool.

Port Grimaud is only a few miles away from St Tropez and we spend a morning exploring this modern, Venetian-style waterway. In 1960 it was just a swamp, and now is a 7-kilometre network of canals, bridges, and colourful houses with 3000 boats moored individually at their doorstep. It's a well-planned settlement, but feels too enclosed for me.

Our stay wouldn't be complete if we didn't have one more day at Nikki Beach. Taking the yacht around to the 3-mile sweep of golden beach, we treat ourselves to an afternoon lying on the huge white mattresses, drinking rosé wine and eating sushi. The credit card gets a 'you only live once' signature, and young Ian and I navigate *Cádiz* back to St Tropez. Ian is in dreamland: he lay next to a beautiful Romanian bare bottom all afternoon.

The beach bars have their own CD music mixes, which are often the latest in electronica and dance music. Move over Dean Martin, we now 'groove' while we sail. Up until now we can only receive BBC Radio on the SSB (single sideband radio), but it's a pleasant change to listen to Riviera Radio 106.5 in English.

This charmed life can last only so long. After a calm night between the Lerins Islands off Cannes, we head back to Antibes. It's young Ian's birthday and we taxi to Juan-les-Pins for dinner on the beach. The tables are set out right to the water's edge, so you can bury your feet in the sand.

Our daughter Janey joins us for a week while *Maximus* sails to Sardinia and young Ian reluctantly leaves. Nice is the capital of the Riviera, and we are lucky to get a berth in Vieux Port, a tiny, quaint marina near the old town. Surrounded by apartments and restaurants that specialise in *moules et frites*, we find the most pleasant marina staff we have dealt with to date. A walk into the old town of Nice is charming, as the buildings haven't changed much since the 1700s.

It's a dog's life here in France as there seem to be no rules for canine companions. When we flew inland I sat next to a dog in a basket that ate the airline meal. You constantly see dogs sitting on laps at restaurants, and they run wild under the stools at bars; consequently you have to watch where you walk on the pavements.

This morning we wake to a thunderstorm, heavy rain and a washed boat. There's nothing like a good storm to clear the air, and now the days are crystal clear. The cottages in Villefranche are wet from the morning downpour, and look vibrant as they bask in the sun.

It takes a lot of talking to get a space in the marina at Monaco. Ian does not take no for an answer. I have never seen so many supercruisers as I have lining the three marinas of this immaculate principality. We are all very lucky to be here.

All dressed up, we walk to the casino square past a dazzling display of white stately buildings, immaculate gardens and streets lined with supercars. The casino is small but dramatic; the odds at the tables don't look good to me, so I watch.

During lunch at the stylish Yacht Club de Monaco, we are surprised to see a model of the Volvo Ocean Race yacht *Merit Cup* in pride of place. We'd forgotten that Grant Dalton had sailed under this yacht club during the race. We owned *Merit Cup* for two years, racing her in Australia. We are tempted to do the ride in a Ferrari around the Grand Prix circuit, but instead quietly stroll around and drink in the sights.

We leave the Italian and French Rivieras with many fond memories, no complaints, and will be back. The people were helpful, the food great and the cruising ground fantastic. And it's no more expensive than anywhere else. Seeing it from the water is a blessing; you can sit back and watch the hustle and bustle on the promenades, then join in if you want to.

Villefranche-sur-Mer

Monaco

Main marina, Monaco

Cliffs, Bonifacio

Bonifacio, Corsica to La Maddalena Archipelago, Sardinia

Our crossing to Corsica is uneventful and we motor-sail 170 miles to Bonifacio in 26 hours. We're now joining up with a previous trip around the Mediterranean – we were here in October 2003; it was very late in the season, with snow dusting the mountains.

Bonifacio is magnificent from the water, with pastel-coloured cliff-top houses and a natural fiord-shaped harbour. Janey leaves us here to join *Maximus* in Porto Cervo. We will join them on September 1 and I'm looking forward to some time on my own while Ian is racing.

Corsica is untouched by developers – its inlets and islands boast rugged, crystal-clear bays. It's also notorious for its wind, so we watch closely for safe anchorages. Rondinara is a bay that features in all advertisements of Corsica. It is a moon-shaped beach with turquoise water, golden sand and fantastic all-round shelter, which gives us time to slow down to do some domestics.

We think we have found paradise until two catamarans full of Australians arrive and the crew on an English boat keep calling out 'What's the cricket score?' (Australia is currently losing to England.) We get invited to a party on the catamaran, and accept before we see *The Castle* banner go up. It's a very noisy night and a host of inflatables trail the catamaran. Even the Italians, with magnum in hand, join in.

It's too much for us so we head out to the island of Cavallo, where the rich and famous have holiday homes and there's a very busy helicopter pad. It looks like a pile of huge boulders were dumped here; some created islands and others

Porto Cervo, Sardinia

lie scattered around the coast. The homes are camouflaged among the stone, and it all looks very natural. As for the lethal boulders in the water, we pay extra attention to the charts.

A mere 8 miles brings us to Sardinia and yet another group of islands. The Archipelago La Maddalena, a series of islands that form a national park, creates a masterpiece of beautiful contrasting colours – red rock, dark blue depths, and sky blue shallows over white sand. Pink Bay adds further to the palette; it's a small, immaculate beach made of unique pink sand. Never before have I visited a beach that is so out of bounds to everyone, even to swim. People were taking the sand, so the authorities banished all unsupervised visits. You can walk around on a wooden platform while being watched by rather officious Italian custodians.

The waterway is full of cruising yachts, but the weather isn't kind to us. Although it's still August, there's the odd cooler night and we hope the summer will stay a little longer. It doesn't stop us swimming and snorkelling in the clear, shallow water. There are more than 40 inlets around the seven islands, covering 49 square kilometres. There's a charge to anchor for every day you are here and for a boat our size it costs €40. The only factor in our favour is that the enforcers of this rule have to find us.

Every bay is another wonderful sight of time-worn granite, and on the eastern side of the islands, the water changes to emerald green. Our favourite islands are Razzoli, Budelli and Santa Maria – they come together to form a star and in the centre is a sheltered passageway.

Maxi yachts waiting to race, Porto Cervo

In port there is the biggest gathering of Maxis in the world, shaping up for a great week of racing. There are 40 boats in three classes and the boats are worth millions.

Porto Cervo, Sardinia

The forecast in Porto Cervo is for beautiful days with a light breeze, and I'm looking forward to seeing 40 Maxis racing in the Maxi Yacht Rolex Cup. Ian will become a Kiwi to race on *Maximus*, and I will sit on the fence. On September 3, two days before racing starts, I'm privileged to be invited by Charles St Clair Brown and Bill Buckley to sail on *Maximus* on a training day. What an experience. The wind was 12 knots and we easily hit 17 knots of boat speed. The 98-footer was so smooth and effortless that it felt like a low-flying aircraft.

In port there is the biggest gathering of Maxis in the world, shaping up for a great week of racing. There are 40 boats in three classes: the fleet of Wally-class boats is the biggest division, ranging from 70 feet to 107 feet, and the boats are worth millions of dollars.

The first race day dawns, and I follow for half the race in the inflatable tender. *Maximus* leads at the finish, but the race is withdrawn because the committee boat forgot to put down a mark on the course. At this level of racing, this should never happen.

The next day, the wind is blowing 23 knots and it isn't long before *Maximus* takes the lead. According to the skipper of *Nariida*, a Norwegian 105-footer, *Maximus* sails past them looking like a trimaran – they can't believe her speed. Leading by miles and looking famous at the last mark, the sky falls in as *Maximus* gybes and the mast breaks. Everything comes down and into the water; millions of dollars are quickly cut away to protect the hull. As Ian later

puts it, 'There was an eerie silence and then an enormous cracking sound as splinters of carbon fibre flew through the air.' No one's injured, and these things do happen, for whatever reason, but it still comes as an enormous shock.

That's the end of the regatta for us. The mast is in two pieces, and the boom and sails are salvaged from 40 metres of water. She will be repaired and racing again next season. This may be the most expensive marina in the Mediterranean, but we are disappointed by their attitude. Unbelievably, when *Maximus* returns from losing her mast we're told she is no longer in the regatta and therefore can't return to her berth where all her equipment is. After a lot of hard talking to staff, this is rectified. It's also uncomfortable for us as they put us on a floating pontoon. On the flip side, the yacht club and surrounds are magnificent, and the quality of yachts and crew competing is mind-blowing.

We are very fortunate while in Sardinia to have the hospitality of our Italian friend Luca, who we met during the Sydney 2000 Olympic Games. His family own a holiday house just north of Porto Cervo, and his mother and sister are very kind in offering us assistance – especially with washing, which is difficult on a yacht. Luca has a very similar lifestyle to ours, except in reverse. He spends summer in Australia and New Zealand on his yacht, and comes back to his house in Torino for the European summer.

Even before the prizegiving for the Maxi Worlds takes place, the Farr 40s and Swan 45s arrive for the Sardinia Rolex Cup. On Sunday we will head to Corsica with Janey.

Pink Beach, Maddalena Islands

Maddalena Islands

View from on high

It's time for me to go up the mast and take some photos, but it's not as easy as I anticipate. My bravado soon disappears and at the first spreaders I can go no further.

Porto Vecchio, Corsica to Rome, Italy

A beautiful day's sail north to Corsica, swapping to the French flag, and we meet our friend Gail Ferguson from Auckland in Porto Vecchio. There's a distinctly autumnal feel in the air as we thread through the Lavezzi islands, sheltering from the wind in an idyllic bay. A cemetery ashore serves as a memorial to a shipwreck when all 750 passengers lost their lives on the way to the Crimean War. It's also a reminder of how dangerous the windy, rocky Strait of Bonifacio can be.

It's time for me to go up the mast and take photos, but it's not as easy as I anticipate. My bravado soon disappears and at the first spreaders I can go no further. I cling to the mast (actually, I can't let go of it); lots of advice comes from the deck below, and the wind picks up. I suddenly admire Ian and anyone else who goes up these things.

Janey will be leaving us in Sardinia to help her friend John Danby sail the 53-foot yacht he skippers down to Malta.

The prospect of having wind on the nose going west up the coast doesn't appeal, so we 'fly' back to Porto Cervo in a fresh breeze and change flags back to Italian. What to do on a wet day? Visit Neolithic ruins. They look just like a pile of rocks, actually, but the lunch on the way home at Dante was great.

Strong winds are predicted from the north-east, so we head for Rome earlier than planned. The night crossing of 130 miles takes 18 hours, under a beautiful moon with lightning on the horizon. Gail and I share several watches, and she's surprised at the number of ships. What starts out as a tiny light on the horizon turns into a huge passenger ship very quickly; some pass quite close by.

The Fiumicino lifting bridge is broken, so we leave *Cádiz* high and dry for eight months at the ACHAB Yacht Club. It's a small marina 20 kilometres from Rome on the Tiber. When *Cádiz* is hauled out, she seems too heavy on one end (possibly the cellar end; one has to leave a little for next year). Gail and I manage a day trip to Rome to visit St Peter's in Vatican City,

but jump queues and accidentally find ourselves looking at the late Pope John Paul II's crypt.

We take the train back to Monaco for the boat show. Ian makes sure I don't get any big ideas around the luxury craft, but I'm just as fascinated by all the designer shoes left on the wharf while buyers view boats. It's great to see so many New Zealanders and Australians promoting their talents.

To Ian's surprise, a piece of history is sitting in the marina. *Gunboat Rangiriri* is the Bruce Farr half-tonner from New Zealand that won the World Half Ton Cup in Sydney in 1977. She brings back many memories as we owned her predecessor, *Titus Canby*, and crossed Cook Strait on her in a gale when I was seven months pregnant. Looking at the 30-footer now, I must have been completely in love or just stupid.

Near the marina are the ruins of the ancient port of Rome, Ostia Antica, where time seems to stand still. Once a thriving port of 100,000 inhabitants in the fourth century BC, it silted up over the centuries until the coastline was two kilometres away. Excavations began in the 16th century, and today you can walk down the original stone roads past temples, the theatre, houses of charioteers, bathhouses, latrines, the marble meat market, and tiled mosaics and the remains of paintings and marble statues. Despite the number of ruins we've already seen in the region we spend hours here, utterly absorbed.

Three seasons in the Med, 8000 miles, 11 countries and lots of friends. Some have asked us which is our favourite country. We don't have one: every country offers something new, from its culture to its history or regional cuisine. Every day, too, brings some new adjustment, and it's deeply satisfying to get out of your comfort zone – to take on a new challenge. Our plans for next year aren't finalised, but we will spend another season in this ancient sea as we're enjoying it immensely. We will revisit some of our favourite places and continue our endless summer.

Acknowledgements

A **big thank you to my family Ian, Janey and Ian Andrew** for all their patience, proofing and support, and for encouraging me to keep writing when the only thing to do while cruising was to eat and sleep; to Di Pearson for publishing on the Internet all my letters (and having a good laugh); and to all the people out there who followed and read every letter. My gratitude goes out to Renée Lang for introducing me to Belinda Cooke and Matt Turner at New Holland Publishers in Auckland; thanks also to the creative team: Trevor Newman, Mary de Ruyter and Charlotte Orr.

First published in 2006 by New Holland Publishers (NZ) Ltd
Auckland • Sydney • London • Cape Town

www.newhollandpublishers.co.nz

218 Lake Road, Northcote, Auckland, New Zealand
14 Aquatic Drive, Frenchs Forest, NSW 2086, Australia
86–88 Edgware Road, London W2 2EA, United Kingdom
80 McKenzie Street, Cape Town 8001, South Africa

Copyright © 2006 in text: Andrea & Ian Treleaven
Copyright © 2006 in photography: Andrea Treleaven
Copyright © 2006 New Holland Publishers (NZ) Ltd

ISBN-13: 978 1 86966 121 2
ISBN-10: 1 86966 121 4

Managing editor: Matt Turner
Designer: Trevor Newman
Editor: Mary de Ruyter
Maps: Pauline Whimp

A catalogue record for this book is available from the National Library of New Zealand

10 9 8 7 6 5 4 3 2 1

Colour reproduction by Pica Digital Pte Ltd, Singapore
Printed by Tien Wah Press (Pte) Ltd